Frommer's®

Zion
AND
Bryce Canyon
National Parks

2nd Edition

by Don & Barbara Laine

IDG Books Worldwide, Inc.
An International Data Group Company
Foster City, CA • Chicago, IL • Indianapolis, IN • New York, NY

IDG BOOKS WORLDWIDE, INC.

An International Data Group Company
919 E. Hillsdale Blvd.
Suite 400
Foster City, CA 94404

Find us online at **www.frommers.com**

ISBN 0-02-863621-X
ISSN 1093-9806

Editor: Margot Weiss
Production Editor: Carol Sheehan
Design by Michele Laseau
Digital Cartography by John Decamillis, Roberta Stockwell
Additional Cartography by Ortelius Design
Photo Editor: Richard Fox
Page Creation: John Bitter and Marie Kristine Parial-Leonardo

Illustrations on pages 152 (Douglas Fir), 157, 159 (Coyote), 160 (Elk, Mule
Deer), 161 (Pronghorn), 164 (American Dipper, Bald Eagle, Golden Eagle),
165 and 168 (Red-Tailed Hawk) by Jasper Burns; illustrations on pages 151,
152 (Juniper), 153, 154, 155, 156, 159 (Chipmunk), 160 (Mountain Lion),
161 (Prairie Dog), 162, 163, 164 (Mountain Chickadee), 166, 167, 168
(Peregrine Falcon), 169, 170, and 171 by Giselle Simons.

SPECIAL SALES

For general information on IDG Books Worldwide's books in the U.S., please call
our Consumer Customer Service department at 1-800-762-2974. For reseller
information, including discounts, bulk sales, customized editions, and premium
sales, please call our Reseller Customer Service department at 1-800-434-3422.

Manufactured in the United States of America

5 4 3 2 1

Contents

4   Hikes & Other Outdoor Pursuits in Zion National Park   55

5   Exploring Bryce Canyon National Park   74

6   Hikes & Other Outdoor Pursuits in Bryce Canyon National Park   87

List of Maps

ABOUT THE AUTHORS

Don and Barbara Laine have written about and traveled extensively throughout the Rocky Mountains and the Southwest. They are the authors of *Frommer's Utah, Frommer's Colorado, Frommer's Denver, Boulder & Colorado Springs,* and *Frommer's Rocky Mountain National Park,* as well as contributors to *Frommer's National Parks of the American West* and *Frommer's USA.*

ACKOWLEDGMENTS

The authors wish to thank for their help: Denny Davies and Dave Rachlis at Zion National Park; Cheryl Schreier and Dave Mecham at Bryce Canyon National Park; Jeanie Linn at Grand Staircase–Escalante National Monument; and Tom Henry at Cedar Breaks National Monument.

AN INVITATION TO THE READER

In researching this book, we discovered many wonderful places—hotels, restaurants, shops, and more. We're sure you'll find others. Please tell us about them, so we can share the information with your fellow travelers in upcoming editions. If you were disappointed with a recommendation, we'd love to know that, too. Please write to:

Frommer's Zion & Bryce Canyon National Parks, 2nd Edition
IDG Travel
1633 Broadway
New York, NY 10019

AN ADDITIONAL NOTE

Please be advised that travel information is subject to change at any time. The publisher and the authors have endeavored to provide useful information in this publication, but we suggest that you write or call ahead for confirmation when making your travel plans. The publisher and authors cannot be held responsible for the experiences of readers while traveling. National parks are, by their very nature, potentially hazardous places. In visiting any of the places or doing any of the activities described herein, readers assume all risk of injury or loss that may accompany such activities. The publisher and the authors disavow all responsibility for injury, death, loss, or property damage that may arise from a reader's visit to any of the places or participation in any of the activities described herein, and the publisher and the authors make no warranties regarding the competence, safety, and reliability of outfitters, tour companies, or training centers described in this publication.

WHAT THE SYMBOLS MEAN
✪ Frommer's Favorites

Our favorite places and experiences—outstanding for quality, value, or both

The following abbreviations are used for credit cards:

AE	American Express	EURO	Eurocard
CB	Carte Blanche	JCB	Japan Credit Bank
DC	Diners Club	MC	MasterCard
DISC	Discover	V	Visa

FIND FROMMER'S ONLINE

Arthur Frommer's Budget Travel Online (www.frommers.com) offers more than 6,000 pages of up-to-the-minute travel information—including the latest bargains and candid, personal articles updated daily by Arthur Frommer himself. No other Web site offers such comprehensive and timely coverage of the world of travel.

Introducing Zion & Bryce Canyon National Parks

*T*here aren't many places in the world where the forces of nature have come together with such dramatic results as in Zion and Bryce Canyon National Parks. From arid desert and desolate canyons, to pine-covered peaks and awe-inspiring rock formations, these two parks—located about 85 miles apart in colorful southern Utah—offer some of the American West's most beautiful scenery, along with almost unlimited opportunities for hiking, camping, and other outdoor experiences.

Zion and Bryce Canyon sit on the vast, high Colorado Plateau. They share this plateau with Utah's three other national parks (Arches, Canyonlands, and Capitol Reef), as well as with Grand Canyon National Park in Arizona, Mesa Verde National Park in Colorado, Chaco Culture National Historical Park in New Mexico, a number of national monuments and state parks, the Hopi Indian reservation, and the vast Navajo Nation, home of America's largest Indian tribe.

The Colorado Plateau developed millions of years ago when forces deep within the earth forced the crust to rise, exposing many strata of rocks. Then nature wielded an artistic touch, using the power of erosion and weathering (over several million more years) to sculpt spectacular rock formations—sometimes delicate and intricate, sometimes bold and stately—and then colored them with an iron-rich palette of reds, oranges, pinks, and browns.

Both Zion and Bryce Canyon National Parks are known for their stunning rock formations—Zion for its massive sandstone monoliths such as the rugged Great White Throne, and Bryce for its more delicate limestone sculptures, like the fanciful Poodle or the stately Sentinel. But it's a mistake to think that the sole reason for visiting the parks is their wondrous natural architecture. You will also find shimmering pools of deep green water, a sometimes-roaring river, forests of pine and fir, broad panoramic views, a vast array of plants and animals, and even a bit of human history, all of which are discussed in the following pages.

Butch Cassidy Slept Here

Robert LeRoy Parker wasn't a bad kid. He was born into a hard-working Mormon family in a southwestern Utah town called Beaver on April 13, 1866. The oldest of 13 children, Robert was a great help to his mother, working on the small ranch his parents bought near Circleville, about 50 miles north of Bryce Canyon.

It was in Circleville where the problems began, when the teenager fell in with some rather unsavory characters, including one Mike Cassidy, who gave the youth his first gun and eventually his last name. Setting out to make his mark in the world, the boy made his way to Telluride, Colorado, worked for one of the mines there for a time, and found himself in Wyoming after a while. A little more wandering took him back to Telluride, and strangely enough the Telluride bank was robbed. Butch Cassidy had officially begun his life of crime.

In the following years, Butch—who gained the nickname after a short stint working in a butcher shop—became expert at rustling cattle, robbing banks, and finally his ultimate glory, robbing trains. Often he and his gang would travel through Utah, hiding out in the desolate badlands, including, it's believed, what is now Bryce Canyon National Park. One story has it that Butch wanted to call his gang the Train Robbers Syndicate, but they raised such hell in celebration of their economic successes that saloon keepers in Vernal and other Utah towns began calling them "that wild bunch," and the name stuck.

One thing that makes both parks so inviting is that they can be experienced in a variety of ways, on many levels. While the adventurer can savor the challenging hiking trails and backcountry routes, the simply curious will relish the unique opportunity to examine millions of years of geologic history, as well as the chance to see rare plants and animals. Meanwhile, those with an artistic bent might totally ignore the recreational and educational aspects of these parks and lose themselves in their beauty. Visitors new to the West may simply want to step back and soak in the total experience.

In searching for the essence of these natural worlds—their rocks, plants, animals, their very being—you'll find well-developed and maintained trail systems, overlooks offering panoramic vistas, interpretative displays, museum programs, and knowledgeable park rangers ready to help you make the most of your visit. At first it seems

Those who have seen the 1969 movie *Butch Cassidy and the Sundance Kid,* with Paul Newman as Butch and Robert Redford as his partner-in-crime Sundance, will recall the spectacular scene in which Butch and his cohorts blow the door off a railroad car, and then use too much dynamite to open the safe, sending bills flying into the air. Apparently it's basically true, having taken place on June 2, 1899 near Wilcox, Wyoming, and according to reports of the day, they got away with $30,000.

The Union Pacific Railroad took exception to Butch's antics, and when the posses started getting a bit too close, Butch, Sundance, and Sundance's lady friend Etta Place took off for South America, where it is said they continued a life of crime for a half-dozen or so years. There are also some stories—unconfirmed—that it was in South America that Butch first killed anyone, that up until that time he had avoided bloodshed whenever possible, believing it was stupid and the result of poor planning.

Then, according to some historians and the movie version of Butch's life, Butch and Sundance were shot dead in a gun battle with army troops in Bolivia. Some, though, believe otherwise—that Butch returned to the United States, visited friends and family in Utah and Wyoming, and eventually settled in Spokane, Washington, where he lived a peaceful and respectable life, under the name William T. Phillips, dying of natural causes in 1937.

overwhelming—how can I possibly see everything there is to be seen here? Don't try. Zion and Bryce Canyon are not to be visited as if they were amusement parks, racing from ride to ride; these natural wonders are to be savored, embraced, and explored, and the best way to do that is to slow down. Take time to ponder the sunrise, sit quietly at the edge of a meadow and wait for a deer to emerge from the woods for its evening meal, and even, as the cliché goes, stop and smell the roses.

It's certain that you won't see every corner of these two parks even on a long vacation of 2 or 3 weeks. Bryce Amphitheater is enormous, filled with countless delightfully shaped and colored formations and groups of formations, with telling names such as Wall Street, Fairyland Canyon, and Queen's Garden. Meanwhile, the rugged stone monuments at Zion, such as the Watchman and the West Temple, are overpowering and tend to underline the insignificance of mankind in the total scheme of things. But among America's western parks, these are two of the easiest to explore, to feel that you've gotten to know their very being. In large part this is because their extensive trail and road systems enable the visitor to explore these parks in fairly small, easily digestible bites, sampling one aspect, letting it settle, and then moving along for another taste.

Bryce Canyon National Park is a bit more user-friendly than Zion, in part because Bryce is more easily defined—it's the hoodoos!—while Zion offers a greater variety of experiences, from river canyons with colorful gardens to rocky windswept ridges. Bryce also has several fairly easy trails that lead right into the middle of some of its best scenery; you start on top of the rim, looking down at these spectacular hoodoos, and within minutes you're among them, looking up. This isn't to say that Zion is hard to get into, but because of the greater variety of terrain it takes a bit more time and effort to achieve that same feeling that you *know* the park.

One interesting difference between the parks is that at Zion the visitor arrives at the bottom of the canyon, and in most cases looks and hikes up toward the rock formations. At Bryce Canyon you arrive at the top, along the rim, and look and then hike down into the amphitheaters. Foot-power is the best way to explore both parks, although those without the physical ability or desire to hike find that there is quite a bit for them to see, as well. Zion has the greatest variety of hiking trails—more than double the number at Bryce—as well as more extreme variations in elevation and terrain. Because Zion is lower, you'll find more favorable hiking conditions in winter there; while summer hikers will appreciate the cooler temperatures in the higher elevations of Bryce Canyon.

1 The Best of Zion & Bryce Canyon National Parks

From their rocky trails to their deep forests, Zion and Bryce Canyon National Parks are enchanting worlds of discovery, spectacular scenic wonders, and magnificent outdoor playgrounds. In fact, the only real problems are choosing what to do, what to see, where to stay, and even where to eat. Because it can be bewildering to try to plan your trip with so many options, we've assembled the very best that these parks and the surrounding areas have to offer—the places and experiences you won't want to miss.

THE BEST DAY HIKES

- **Emerald Pools Trail System** (Zion National Park): If green is your color, you'll love this trail—algae keeps the three pools glowing a deep, rich, and yes, emerald green. The first part of the trail leads through a forest to the Lower Emerald Pool, with its lovely waterfall and hanging garden. See chapter 4.

- **East Mesa Trail** (Zion National Park): Allow a full day for this 6-mile hike, which is an easier and shorter route, through ponderosa pines and manzanita, to Observation Point than the Observation Point Trail. From the promontory you'll get spectacular views down Zion Canyon, with the Great White Throne in the foreground and Red Arch Mountain beyond. See chapter 4.

- **Navajo Loop/Queen's Garden Trail** (Bryce Canyon National Park): To truly experience magical Bryce Canyon, you should hike down into it, and this not-too-difficult combination trail is the perfect way to go. Start at Sunset Point and get the steepest part out of the way first. You'll pass Thor's Hammer and wonder why it hasn't fallen, ponder the towering skyscrapers of Wall Street, and visit with some of the park's most fanciful formations, including majestic Queen Victoria herself. See chapter 6.

- **Rim Trail** (Bryce Canyon National Park): This underrated trail is a delight, providing splendid views down into spectacularly scenic Bryce Amphitheater from a variety of vantage points over its 5^1/$_2$-mile length. More walking than hiking, the Rim Trail includes a half-mile section between two overlooks—Sunrise and Sunset—that is suitable for wheelchairs. Views are especially fine early in the morning, when you can watch the changing light on the red rocks below. See chapter 6.

THE BEST BACKCOUNTRY HIKES

- **Hiking the Narrows** (Zion National Park): This is an experience unique to Zion National Park—a 1,000-foot-deep canyon, with water filling it from side to side in most places. Although much of Zion is dry rock, this is anything but, and is an incredible experience for those in good shape and with strong nerves. It can be experienced in three ways—as a short day hike, full-day hike, or an overnight hike—but all involve getting wet. *Warning:* Because the Narrows is prone to flash flooding, check weather forecasts carefully before setting out. See chapter 4.

- **Riggs Spring Loop Trail** (Bryce Canyon National Park): Although this 9-mile loop can be hiked in 1 day, it's better as an overnight backpacking trip. This enables you to take your time to see wildlife, and possibly even get a glimpse of a mountain lion, as you hike through forests of Douglas fir, ponderosa pines, piñons, and aspen, with views of the white and pink cliffs soaring above. See chapter 6.

THE BEST WILDLIFE VIEWING SPOTS

- **Hiking the Angels Landing Trail** (Zion National Park): This difficult hike provides opportunities to see mule deer, golden eagles, peregrine falcons, and lizards; it also offers splendid views into Zion Canyon. *Warning:* The last half mile of this trail is along a knife-edge ridge—*definitely* not for anyone with a fear of heights. See chapter 4.

- **The Riverside Walk** (Zion National Park): Water attracts wildlife, and here, deep in a slot canyon carved by the Virgin River, you're apt to see the American dipper—also called the water ouzel—as it dives into the water in search of aquatic insects. This is also the only place in the world where you'll find the Zion snail, although it may be hard to recognize, since it is only $^1/_8$ inch across. *Warning:* Because the Narrows is prone to flash flooding, check weather forecasts carefully before setting out. See chapters 4 and 10.

- **Weeping Rock Area** (Zion National Park): Easily accessible via a short but steep paved trail, Weeping Rock oozes water that nurtures lush hanging gardens and produces the perfect habitat for a variety of wildlife, especially birds. Watch for peregrine falcons, American dippers, canyon wrens, and white-throated swifts. See chapters 4 and 10.

- **Riggs Spring Loop Trail** (Bryce Canyon National Park): This little-used backcountry trail through a woodland provides an opportunity to see a variety of wildlife, possibly even one of the park's elusive mountain lions. See chapters 6 and 10.

- **Campgrounds** (both Zion and Bryce Canyon National Parks): It couldn't be easier to see wildlife. Simply sit quietly at your campsite, preferably when few people are in the campground, and wait. You'll see Uinta chipmunks in both parks, white-tailed antelope squirrels at Zion, and golden-mantled ground squirrels at Bryce Canyon. There are almost always plenty of birds, and you're also apt to see mule deer, especially in Watchman Campground at Zion National Park. See chapters 7 and 10.

THE BEST SCENIC VIEWS

- **Zion Canyon Road** (Zion National Park): The 14-mile drive through Zion Canyon is impressive no matter how you do it—in your own vehicle (in winter only) or on the shuttle from spring through fall. In every direction the views are awe-inspiring, as the massive stone formations reach for the heavens. The road also provides easy access to a number of wonderful viewpoints and trailheads just off the roadway. See chapter 3.

- **Angels Landing Trail** (Zion National Park): The strenuous Angels Landing Trail leads across a high narrow ridge to a spectacular and dizzying view of Zion Canyon. *Warning:* The last half mile of this trail is along a knife-edge ridge—*definitely* not for anyone with a fear of heights. See chapter 4.

- **The Narrows** (Zion National Park): The sheer 1,000-foot-high walls are awe-inspiring, almost frightening, as they enclose you in a narrow world of hanging gardens, waterfalls, and sculpted sandstone arches, with the Virgin River pouring over and around your feet and legs. The Narrows are too narrow to allow you to walk next to the river, so you have to wade right through it—but the views make it worth getting wet. *Warning:* Because the Narrows is prone to flash flooding, check weather forecasts carefully before setting out. See chapter 4.

- **Inspiration Point** (Bryce Canyon National Park): An appropriately named stop, Inspiration Point provides a phenomenal view down into Bryce Amphitheater, the park's largest and most colorful natural amphitheater. From here you see the Silent City, packed with hoodoos and inspiring to the imagination. Some claim the view is even better just south of Inspiration Point along the Rim Trail, up a little rise, at what is usually called Upper Inspiration Point. See chapters 5 and 6.

- **The Queen's Garden Trail** (Bryce Canyon National Park): Presided over by majestic Queen Victoria, these thousands of colorful and intricately sculpted spires present a magnificent display when viewed from the rim. From the trail below, they're even better. See chapters 5 and 6.

- **The Rim at Sunrise** (Bryce Canyon National Park): If you thought the hoodoos were magnificent in the full light of day, wait until you see them reflecting the deep colors of the morning sun as it rises slowly above the rim. The changing angle of light creates a constantly moving panorama of shadow and color.

Walk along the Rim Trail or stop at the viewpoints along the northern half of the park's scenic drive. See chapters 5 and 6.

THE BEST NATURAL SPECTACLES

- **The Great White Throne** (Zion National Park): A huge white monolith, the Great White Throne demands attention no matter when you first glimpse it. Considered the symbol of Zion National Park, this massive block of Navajo sandstone towers 2,000 feet high, and can be seen from the scenic drive as well as from several hiking trails, including Observation Point Trail, Deertrap Mountain Trail, Angels Landing Trail, and Emerald Pools Trail. See chapters 3 and 4.

- **The Narrows** (Zion National Park): It's difficult to comprehend that this beautiful canyon, 1,000 feet deep and less than 30 feet wide in places, was carved from solid stone, beginning millions of years ago, by the often gently flowing Virgin River at your feet. But to see the flip side of the river, just wait for a rainstorm, and it becomes an angry, destructive force that you can well imagine would slice through anything that got in its way. *Warning:* Because the Narrows is prone to flash flooding, check weather forecasts carefully before setting out. See chapter 4.

- **Queen Victoria** (Bryce Canyon National Park): Among the most impressive hoodoos in the park, from the right angle this honestly looks just like the photos of England's Queen Victoria you see in books and magazines. It even has the same air of superiority. See chapter 6.

- **Bryce Amphitheater Capped with Snow** (Bryce Canyon National Park): The hoodoos become transformed into intricately carved creatures topped with white icing, a fairyland in orange and white. You'll get great views either from stops along the scenic drive or by walking the Rim Trail. See chapters 5 and 6.

THE BEST WINTER SPORTS LOCATION

- **Fairyland Loop Trail** (Bryce Canyon National Park): There aren't many cross-country ski trails that can match Bryce Canyon's Fairyland Loop for scenic beauty. The section of the hiking trail that is open to cross-country skiers leads 1 mile through a pine and juniper forest to the Fairyland Point Overlook, with its spectacular views into Bryce Amphitheater, where a blanket of snow adorns the multicolored hoodoos with a sparkling white mantle. See chapters 5 and 6.

THE BEST HISTORIC SITE

- **Bryce Canyon Lodge** (Bryce Canyon National Park): Built by the Union Pacific Railroad and opened in 1924, this handsome sandstone and ponderosa pine lodge with its large stone fireplace in the lobby has been faithfully restored to its 1920s appearance. The lobby contains historic photos taken in the park during that period. See chapter 5.

THE BEST CHILDREN'S & FAMILY EXPERIENCES

- **Junior Ranger Program** (Zion National Park): Although Junior Ranger programs are available at most national parks, the one offered at Zion each summer is quite extensive, with both morning and afternoon activities that teach kids what makes this natural wonder so special. See chapter 3.
- **Weeping Rock Trail** (Zion National Park): This short hike on a paved trail has interpretive signs explaining the natural history of the area as it wanders through a mixed forest. But the best part is at the end, when the trail arrives at a rock alcove with lush hanging gardens of ferns and wildflowers, where you can lift your face to receive a cooling spray of mist from above. See chapter 4.
- **Queen's Garden Trail** (Bryce Canyon National Park): Not only is this trail fairly easy, but it drops down into one of the most scenic parts of the park, meandering among some of the park's most unique and oddly carved hoodoos. It's fun to let your imagination run wild, both for youngsters and the kid in all of us. See chapter 6.

THE BEST DRIVE-IN CAMPING

- **Watchman Campground** (Zion National Park): Located just inside the park's south entrance, Watchman Campground has well-spaced sites, lots of trees, and that national park atmosphere you came here to enjoy. In addition, this campground is right on

Movie Trivia

Most of the dozens of Western movies filmed in Utah were done in either Monument Valley or the Moab area, both famous for their classic American West scenery. However, the epic Western *The Big Trail,* one of John Wayne's first roles as a leading man, was shot at Zion National Park in 1930.

the Pa'rus Trail, providing easy access to practically the entire park. See chapters 4 and 7.

- **North Campground** (Bryce Canyon National Park): While both of Bryce Canyon National Park's campgrounds offer plenty of trees providing that genuine "forest camping" experience, North Campground is closer to the Rim Trail than the park's other campground, making it easier to rush over to catch those amazing sunrise colors. See chapter 7.
- **Ruby's Inn RV Park & Campground** (near Bryce Canyon National Park; ☎ **435/834-5301**): For those who want full RV hookups, a woodsy camping experience, lots of amenities, and easy access to the national park, this is the place to be. Part of a giant complex containing a motel, shops, swimming pools, and all sorts of other attractions and activities, this campground has trees and open space as well. See chapter 7.

THE BEST BACKCOUNTRY CAMPING

- **La Verkin Creek/Kolob Arch Trails** (Zion National Park): You'll have to sign up in advance for one of the isolated campsites along this spectacularly scenic trail in the Kolob Canyons. The trail takes you through forests of conifers, cottonwoods, and box elders, past both hanging gardens and a series of waterfalls. There is also a side trip to a view of Kolob Arch—at over 300 feet wide, one of the largest natural arches in the world. See chapter 4.

THE BEST LODGING IN & NEAR THE PARKS

- **Zion Lodge** (Zion National Park; ☎ **435/772-3213**): The handsome Zion Lodge was built by the Union Pacific Railroad, but tragedy struck in 1966 when it was destroyed by fire. However, it was rebuilt the following year in its original style, and continues to offer the best location for this park's visitors. Situated in a forest with spectacular views of the park's rock cliffs, it offers both cabins and motel rooms. The charming cabins, each with a private porch, stone (gas-burning) fireplace, two double beds, and log beams just seem like the right place to stay in the park. See chapter 7.
- **Bryce Canyon Lodge** (Bryce Canyon National Park; ☎ **435/834-5361**): This handsome sandstone and ponderosa pine lodge is the perfect place to stay while visiting the park. Opened in 1924, it has all the atmosphere of the 1920s, but with most of

the modern conveniences people today expect. Especially recommended are its delightful cabins, which have been authentically restored and contain gas-burning stone fireplaces. Those wanting a bit more elegance will enjoy one of the lodge's suites, which are decorated with white wicker furnishings and have ceiling fans and separate sitting areas. Very fancy. See chapter 7.

- **Flanigan's Inn** (near Zion National Park; ☎ 800/765-7787 or 435/772-3244): Made of natural wood and rock, and set among trees, lawns, and flowers just outside the entrance to Zion National Park, this attractive complex has a mountain lodge atmosphere. It's a place where you might actually want to spend some time—unlike some other area options, which are just good places to crash at the end of a busy day. See chapter 8.

- **Snow Family Guest Ranch** (near Zion National Park; ☎ 800/308-7669 or 435/635-2500): A peaceful horse ranch about 12 miles west of Zion National Park's south entrance, this is a welcome alternative to the hustle-and-bustle of the motels at the park entrance. Rooms are individually decorated with a western flair and have log furnishings. The large bridal suite has a massive log bed, claw-foot tub, and a separate shower. Guided scenic trail rides are offered for an additional charge. See chapter 8.

- **Best Western Ruby's Inn** (near Bryce Canyon National Park; ☎ 435/834-5341): The motel rooms here are fine—clean and well-maintained, with color TVs, telephones, and air-conditioning—but the real reason to stay here is the location, just outside the park entrance. Numerous amenities are offered, from swimming pools and restaurants to shuttle services and plane rides. See chapter 8.

- **Bryce Point Bed & Breakfast** (near Bryce Canyon National Park; ☎ 435/679-8629): The five rooms at this B&B are all unique, each decorated and named for one of Lamar and Ethel LeFevre's children. Consequently, there's a firefighter's room, a commercial airline room, and so forth, all done tastefully and attractively. Most rooms offer beautiful views of Bryce Point through large picture windows, and there is also a handsomely furnished honeymoon cottage. See chapter 8.

THE BEST RESTAURANTS IN & NEAR THE PARKS

- **Zion Lodge** (Zion National Park; ☎ 435/772-3213): You can't beat the view here—large picture windows face the park's magnificent rock formations—and the food is pretty special, too. Try the slow-roasted prime rib au jus or the very popular Utah red mountain trout. See chapter 7.

- **Bryce Canyon Lodge** (Bryce Canyon National Park; ☎ **435/ 834-5361**): A delightful mountain lodge atmosphere and excellent food make the Bryce Canyon Lodge Dining Room a winner. Decorated with American Indian weavings and baskets, and a gigantic 1897 American flag, the restaurant has two large stone fireplaces and picture windows looking out at the park. The menu here is similar to that at the Zion Lodge (both run by the same concessionaire), with house specialties of slow-roasted prime rib au jus and fresh mountain trout, plus chicken dishes and vegetarian items. Then there are the lodge's specialty ice creams and desserts, such as the exotic and very tasty wild "Bryceberry" crumb cake (you won't get that at Zion!). See chapter 7.
- **The Bit & Spur Restaurant & Saloon** (near Zion National Park; ☎ **435/772-3498**): Although this looks like a rough-and-tumble Old West saloon at first glance, it's really a very fine restaurant, similar to one of the better restaurants in Santa Fe. The menu includes Mexican standards such as burritos, flautas, and traditional chile stew; but you'll also find more exotic creations. Portions are generous, too. See chapter 8.

THE BEST SIDE TRIPS

- **Cedar Breaks National Monument** (near Cedar City, a side trip from Zion National Park): A delightful little park, Cedar Breaks National Monument is a junior Bryce Canyon, with a spectacular natural amphitheater filled with stone spires, arches, and columns, and painted in ever-changing reds, purples, oranges, and ochres. Here you can also camp among the spruce, firs, and wildflowers that blanket the 10,000-foot plateau each summer. See chapter 9.
- **Grand Staircase–Escalante National Monument** (near Bryce Canyon National Park): Among America's newest national monuments, this vast wilderness covering some 1.7 million acres is known for its stark, rugged beauty, and particularly its red-orange canyons and deep river valleys. Unlike most other national monuments, almost all of this sweeping area is undeveloped— there are few all-weather roads, only one maintained hiking trail, and two small developed campgrounds. But for the adventurous, there are miles upon miles of dirt roads and practically unlimited opportunities for hiking, horseback riding, camping, and exploring. See chapter 9.

2 A Look at Zion

While it may be easy to conjure up a single defining image of the enormous Grand Canyon or the delicately sculpted rock hoodoos of Bryce, Zion is more difficult to pin down. Here you'll find a collage of images and secrets, an entire smorgasbord of experiences, sights, and even smells, from massive stone sculptures and monuments to lush forests and roaring rivers. Zion is a park to explore, not merely see; take time to walk its trails, visit viewpoints at different times of the day to see the changing light, and let the park work its magic on you.

First established as Mukuntuweap National Monument in 1909—*mukuntuweap* is a Paiute Indian word meaning "straight arrow"—its name was changed to Zion National Monument in 1918, and the area gained national park status the following year. Comprising more than 147,000 acres, the park covers a wide range of elevations—from 3,700 feet to 8,726 feet above sea level—and terrain that runs the gamut from desert to forest, with a dramatic river canyon known as the Narrows thrown in for good measure.

These extremes of elevation have resulted in extremes of climate as well—temperatures in the desert areas soar to well over 100°F in the summer, while higher elevations are sometimes covered with snow and ice in the winter. Due to this variety of conditions, Zion harbors a vast array of plant life, ranging from cactus and yucca to ponderosa pines and cottonwoods. In fact, with almost 800 native species, Zion National Park is said to have the richest diversity of plants in Utah. Be sure to watch for hanging gardens, watered from porous rocks, which you'll see clinging to the sides of cliffs.

Zion is also home to a great variety of animals, drawn here in large part by the year-round water source. Indigenous mammals range from pocket gophers to mountain lions; but you'll also spy hundreds of birds, lizards of all shapes and sizes, and a dozen species of snakes. (Only the Great Basin rattlesnake is poisonous, and it usually slithers away from you faster than you can run from it.) Mule deer are commonly observed grazing along the forest edges, and practically every park visitor comes across squirrels and chipmunks. A few shy elk and bighorn sheep may surface, although they're seldom seen. Among the creatures unique to the park is the tiny Zion snail.

Of course, it's not only plants and animals that need water. For some 1,500 years, humans have come here seeking not only water but also the plants and animals that the water nurtures. There is

Impressions

evidence that a group of people known as the Basket Makers lived here as early as A.D. 500, hunting the area's wildlife, gathering berries and seeds, and growing corn, squash, and other crops. They apparently abandoned the area about A.D. 1200, perhaps because of climate changes. Members of the American Indian tribe called the Paiutes—whose descendants still live in southern Utah—are believed to have spent time in what is now the national park, but built no permanent homes. Spanish explorers were in the area in the late 18th century, and American fur traders came in the early 19th century, but there is no evidence that either actually entered Zion Canyon.

Historians believe that it was not until the 1850s that European-Americans finally ventured into Zion Canyon. Probably the first was Mormon pioneer Nephi Johnson, who was shown Zion Canyon by Paiutes in November 1858, and for whom Johnson Mountain is named. He was among a group of members of the Church of Jesus Christ of Latter-day Saints that was sent from Salt Lake City, by church leader Brigham Young, in search of arable land. By the early 1860s, the Mormons had begun to establish farms and ranches in the area, near where Zion Lodge is located today and at other locations in what is now the national park. It was early Mormon settler Isaac Behunin who is credited with naming his homestead "Little Zion," because it seemed to him to be a bit of heaven on earth.

In the 1870s, Major John Wesley Powell explored the area, describing in his journals Angels Landing, Court of the Patriarchs, and some of the park's other now-famous landmarks. At about the same time, surveyor G. K. Gilbert was mapping southern Utah. He named the Narrows and described it as "the most wonderful defile it has been my fortune to behold."

Today, Zion National Park casts a spell over you as you gaze upon its sheer multicolored walls of sandstone, explore its narrow canyons, search for hanging gardens of ferns and wildflowers, or listen to the roar of the churning, tumbling Virgin River. Many things to many people, Zion National Park might be a day hike down a narrow canyon, a rugged climb up the face of a massive stone monument, or the quiet appreciation of the red glow of sunset over majestic peaks.

3 A Look at Bryce Canyon

One of America's most scenic destinations, Bryce Canyon National Park is a magical land, a place of inspiration and spectacular beauty where thousands of intricately shaped rock formations stir the imagination, as they stand silent watch in their colorful cathedrals. But, perhaps even more important, Bryce Canyon is also one of the West's most accessible national parks. Several trails lead down into the canyon—technically what geologists call an amphitheater—making it relatively easy to get to know this beautiful jewel up close. In addition, there's an easy Rim Trail, part of which is wheelchair accessible, that makes many of the park's best views available to virtually everyone.

The smallest of Utah's five national parks, with an area of just under 36,000 acres, Bryce Canyon was declared a national monument by Pres. Warren Harding in 1923. The following year the U.S. Congress passed provisional legislation to create Utah National Park, and in 1928 Congress finalized the change in status and renamed it Bryce Canyon National Park, in honor of one of its early residents. The park ranges in elevation from 6,620 to 9,115 feet, with desert terrain of piñon, juniper, sagebrush, and cactus at the lower levels; and a cool high country consisting of a dense forest of fir, spruce, and even ancient bristlecone pines. In between, where the campgrounds and visitor center are located, is a ponderosa pine forest.

Bryce Canyon is best known for its hoodoos, which geologists tell us are simply pinnacles of rock, often oddly shaped, left standing after millions of years of water and wind erosion. But perhaps a more interesting explanation lies in a Paiute legend. These American Indians, who lived in the area for several hundred years before being forced out by Anglo pioneers, told of a "Legend People" who lived here in the old days. The powerful Coyote turned them to stone for their evil ways, and even today they remain frozen in time.

Whatever the cause, Bryce Canyon is delightfully unique. Its intricate and often whimsical formations are smaller and on a more human scale than the impressive rocks seen at nearby Zion, and Bryce Canyon is far easier to explore than the sometimes intimidating vastness of Grand Canyon National Park. Bryce is comfortable and inviting in its beauty; we feel we know it simply by gazing over the rim, and we're on intimate terms after just one morning on the trail.

Although the colorful hoodoos are the first things that grab your attention, it isn't long before you notice the deep amphitheaters that

---

Such glorious tints, such keen contrasts of light and shade . . . can never be forgotten . . . This is one of the grand panoramas of the plateau country.

—Geologist Clarence Dutton (1880)

---

enfold them, with their cliffs, windows, and arches—all colored in shades of red, brown, orange, yellow, and white—that change and glow with the rising and setting sun. Beyond the rocks and light are the other faces of the park: three separate life zones, each with its own unique vegetation, changing with elevation; and a kingdom of animals, from the busy chipmunks and ground squirrels to stately mule deer and their archenemy, the mountain lion. Also sometimes present in the more remote areas of the park are elk and pronghorn.

It's not known if prehistoric cultures actually saw the wonderful hoodoos at Bryce Canyon, although archeologists do know Paleo-Indians hunted in the area some 15,000 years ago. By about A.D. 700, the Basket Makers had established small villages in Paria Valley, east of Bryce Canyon in what is now Grand Staircase–Escalante National Monument, also discussed in this book (see chapter 9). By about A.D. 1100, ancestral Puebloan peoples (also called the Anasazi) were living east of Bryce Canyon, and are believed to have visited what is now the park in search of game and timber.

However, serious exploration of the Bryce area likely began later, with the Paiutes; and it's possible that trappers, prospectors, and early Mormon scouts may have visited here in the early to mid-1800s, before Major John Wesley Powell conducted the first thorough survey of the region in the early 1870s. Shortly after Powell's exploration—in 1875—Mormon pioneer Ebenezer Bryce, a Scottish carpenter, and his wife Mary moved here and tried raising cattle. Their home became known as "Bryce's Canyon." Although they stayed only 5 years before moving to Arizona, Bryce's legacy is his name and his oft-quoted description of the canyon as "a helluva place to lose a cow."

2

Planning Your Trip

*T*here once was a time when planning a visit to a national park—particularly those in the western United States—involved little more than choosing the dates and packing the car. You could be assured there would be campsites available, and you usually had the luxury of waiting until you arrived to decide exactly what you wanted to do. Those days are mostly gone; today the wise traveler invests a bit of time before leaving home, not only by reading such books as this one, but also by contacting park offices for maps and information, checking out lodging and camping choices, making reservations, and even researching restaurant, shopping, and side-trip possibilities.

There are several reasons for this. First and foremost is that as more people—from this country and the world over—discover the parks, the more crowded they get and the harder it becomes to secure campsites, lodging, and even parking. To combat this, it's best to decide what you want to do at the park and then try to schedule your visit for the least-crowded time that is best for those activities. For instance, as you'll discover in the following chapters, guided horseback rides are only offered during warmer months, but these are also the busiest times at both Zion and Bryce Canyon National Parks. Therefore, if horseback riding is something you want to do, schedule your trip for spring or fall—what people in the tourism industry call the shoulder seasons—when stables are open, but before or after the busy summer season.

Another good reason for advance planning is that you don't want to waste precious vacation time searching for a motel or campsite vacancy. Luckily, there are far more lodging and dining choices in and near the national parks than there were even 10 or 20 years ago. At that time, we were happy if we found a restaurant that was clean and served basic American food. Today the choices are phenomenal, and dining out has evolved from simply filling the stomach into an important part of the national park vacation experience.

So don't dread the planning work—like the anticipation of and preparation for a birthday party, Christmas, or other special event, planning a trip to a national park can be a load of fun.

1   Getting Started: Information & Reservations

Start at the national park offices for information on what to see and do, and for current warnings or changes that might not be included in this book, such as road or trail closures.

For advance information on what to see and do in **Zion National Park,** contact the Superintendent, Zion National Park, Springdale, UT 84767-1099 (☎ **435/772-3256;** www.nps.gov/zion). It's best to write at least a month before your planned visit, and specify what type of information you need. Officials request that those seeking trip-planning information write rather than call, leaving the phone lines open for those needing current and changeable information such as hiking trail conditions and closures.

You can also purchase books, maps, and videos from the non-profit **Zion Natural History Association,** Zion National Park, Springdale, UT 84767 (☎ **800/635-3959** or 435/772-3264). Some publications are available in foreign languages, and several videos can be purchased in either VHS or PAL formats. Those wanting to help the nonprofit association can join ($15 single or $25 family annually) and get a 20% discount on purchases, plus lesser discounts at many other national park bookstores.

For advance information on what to see and do in **Bryce Canyon National Park,** contact the Superintendent, Bryce Canyon National Park, P.O. Box 170001, Bryce Canyon, UT 84717, or call weekdays between 8am and 4:30pm mountain time (☎ **435/834-5322;** www.nps.gov/brca). It's best to write at least a month before your planned visit, and specify the kind of information you require.

If you desire even more details to help plan your trip, you can order books, maps, posters, and videos (in VHS and PAL formats) from the nonprofit **Bryce Canyon Natural History Association,** Bryce Canyon, UT 84717 (☎ **888/362-2642**). The association does not offer memberships, but does give a discount to current members of other national park natural history associations.

LODGING & CAMPING   Both Zion and Bryce Canyon Lodges, which are among the best places to stay while visiting these parks, are usually booked months in advance, especially for the busy summer season, and even the basic motels in the parks' gateway towns are often full. Therefore it's best to make lodging reservations as early as possible. Reservations are recommended for those planning to stay at commercial campgrounds in the gateway towns for both parks, especially if you'll be arriving in the late afternoon or

Southwestern Utah

19

evening. Reservations are not accepted at National Park Service campgrounds at Bryce Canyon, but a reservations system has been implemented at one campground in Zion.

USEFUL PUBLICATIONS   Although we have tried to pack as much information as possible into this book, you may want additional information before your trip, especially if you are particularly interested in the area's geology or wildlife, or plan to do a lot of backpacking. The nonprofit natural history associations in both parks (see above) can provide numerous publications, from books to brochures to maps, that will help you plan your park visit. You'll find detailed trail descriptions covering both parks in *Hiking Zion & Bryce Canyon National Parks* (Helena, Montana: Falcon Press, 1997), by Erik Molvar and Tamara Martin.

Among publications available from the **Zion Natural History Association** are the easy-to-understand 22-page booklet *An Introduction to the Geology of Zion National Park*, by Al Warneke; and *Exploring the Backcountry of Zion National Park: Off-trail Routes*, by Thomas Brereton and James Dunaway. The association also publishes a very useful pocket-size hiking guide, *Zion—The Trails*, compiled by Bob Lineback. Those planning to spend a lot of time on the trails and in the backcountry will want to purchase a copy of the association's topographic map.

The **Bryce Canyon Natural History Association** is a good source for books and maps as well, including the hiking guide mentioned above, *Hiking Zion & Bryce Canyon National Parks*. Published by the association is *The Bryce Canyon Auto and Hiking Guide*, by Tully Stroud and Paul R. Johnson, with discussions of the various viewpoints and hiking trails, and a variety of color photos of the park plus historic black-and-white photos. For those seeking more details on the park's geology, the association publishes *Shadows of Time, The Geology of Bryce Canyon National Park*, 1994, by Frank DeCourten, John Telford, and Hannah Hinchman.

Those planning other stops in Utah during their visit to these national parks should consider purchasing *Frommer's Utah*, also by Don and Barbara Laine, the authors of this book.

2 When to Go

There are a number of factors to consider in choosing when to visit Zion and Bryce Canyon National Parks, including weather, crowds, and activities. Of course, those with children in school will usually have their travel schedules dictated by the school calendar, which means they will be visiting the parks at their busiest times—when everybody else with kids is visiting. But this is not necessarily bad. Both parks offer by far the largest number of children's activities during school summer vacations, and joining these ranger-led programs will enable your children to meet other kids and possibly make new friends. And what kid wants to hang out with his boring old parents all the time, anyway?

Another consideration is lodging. Rates at and near both parks are higher—sometimes considerably higher—in summer. However, visitors also have more choices in summer since some properties, including the wonderful Bryce Canyon Lodge, close in winter. See chapter 7, "Where to Stay & Eat in the Parks" and chapter 8, "Gateway Towns," for complete lodging and dining information.

THE CLIMATES

Although Zion and Bryce Canyon National Parks are in the same general area—in southern Utah on the Colorado Plateau—there are differences in climate, mainly as a result of differences in elevation. Zion ranges from 3,700 feet to 8,726 feet, while the elevation at Bryce Canyon starts at 6,620 and rises to 9,115 feet.

Both parks experience all four seasons, although the winters at Zion are relatively mild and little snow falls in the canyon. Weatherwise, spring and fall are the best times to visit Zion, with temperatures ranging from lows in the 40s to pleasant highs in the 80s. Summer daytime highs often soar well above 100°F, with lows dipping only into the 70s. During this time, hiking is best done in the early mornings, especially considering the frequent afternoon thunderstorms in July and August that can change a babbling brook into a raging torrent in minutes.

Because of its higher elevation, Bryce Canyon is almost always cooler than Zion. From May to October, daytime temperatures are pleasant—usually from the low 60s to the upper 80s—while nights are cool, dropping into the 40s even at the height of summer. Afternoon thunderstorms are common in July and August. During winter, days are generally clear and crisp, with high temperatures often reaching the 40s, while nights are cold, usually in the single digits or teens, and it is not uncommon to see temperatures well below zero. Snow is common in winter, although park staff plow the roads to the viewpoints.

In both parks, weather conditions may limit some activities at certain times. For instance, at Zion you'll want to avoid long hikes in midsummer, when the park bakes under temperatures that can exceed a sizzling 100°F; and at Bryce Canyon, hiking on steep trails can be dangerous during and immediately after winter storms, when ice and snow can make trails slick and treacherous.

AVOIDING THE CROWDS

Both parks get their highest visitation in summer—particularly during school vacations, from early June to mid-August—and those who want to avoid crowds should try to visit at other times.

Zion receives almost half its annual visitors from June to August, while its quietest months are December, January, and February. Of course, even at relatively warm Zion it's chilly then, and there is the possibility that you may have to contend with some snow and ice (although it rarely lasts). If your schedule permits, many consider it a good compromise to visit in April, May, September, or October, when the weather is usually good but the park is less crowded.

Although Bryce Canyon National Park receives only two-thirds the number of annual visitors that pour into nearby Zion National Park, Bryce can still be crowded, especially during its peak season from mid-June to August, when the campgrounds are often full by 2pm. A better time to visit, if your schedule allows, is spring or fall. If you don't mind a bit of cold and snow, the park is practically deserted in the winter—a typical January sees some 22,000 to 25,000 visitors, while in August there are well over 10 times that number—and the sight of bright red hoodoos capped with fresh white snow is something you won't soon forget.

At both parks, there are two other ways to avoid crowds at almost any time of year. First, get started on your explorations as early as possible in the day—preferably just after sunrise. Not only is the light best then and the chances of seeing wildlife much better than later in the day, but you'll practically have the park to yourself, since the majority of visitors don't usually get going until about 10am.

The second way to avoid crowds is simply to walk away from them. It's sad but true that most visitors never venture far from the major viewpoints, and their loss can be your gain. You can have a wonderful solitary experience if you're just willing to expend a little energy. Among the lesser-used day hikes at Bryce Canyon are Fairyland Loop and Peekaboo Loop; and at Zion try the Hop Valley and Observation Point Trails. (See chapter 4 for more day hikes in Zion and chapter 6 for more day hikes at Bryce Canyon.)

At Zion you can also avoid hordes of tourists by spending time in Kolob Canyons, in the far northwest section of the park; it's spectacular and receives surprisingly little use, at least in comparison to

A British Invasion

Summer visitors to Zion National Park who want a change of pace can step back to Elizabethan England. It's a much shorter trip than you might think, only 60 miles north to the community of Cedar City, where Utah's premier theater event, the **Utah Shakespearean Festival,** takes place each year from mid-June to mid-October.

The Bard's plays have been professionally staged in this unlikely setting since 1962, and the festival has been going strong and getting better ever since. Each summer there are six plays—usually three by Shakespeare plus three others—presented with top actors in true Elizabethan style, in an open-air replica of the original Globe Theatre. If it rains, productions are moved into an adjacent enclosed theater. Then there are two additional plays presented during the festival's fall season, which runs from mid-September to mid-October. Ticket prices range from $11 to $40.

The plays are only part of the fun, however. "Royal Feastes," complete with medieval entertainment and winsome serving wenches, are held several evenings each week; the Elizabethan-style prix fixe dinner is $30 per person. Backstage tours are offered Monday through Saturday for $7 per person. A variety of other programs, including literary seminars and workshops, are also offered.

The festival takes place on the Southern Utah University campus at 351 W. Center St., Cedar City, UT 84720. Contact the festival office (☎ **800/752-9849** or 435/586-7878; fax 435/586-1944; www.bard.org).

Zion Canyon. To really get away from humanity at Bryce Canyon, head out on one of the park's two backcountry trails. As noted above, see chapters 4 and 6, which describe the hiking trails and other outdoor activities at each park.

SEASONAL EVENTS

Most of the ranger-led activities, such as campfire and amphitheater programs and guided hikes and walks, occur during the summer, although a few are scheduled year-round, such as the once-a-month star-watching program presented at Bryce Canyon by astronomers from Hansen Planetarium in Salt Lake City. Check the bulletin boards at park visitor centers for current information.

In the Bryce Canyon area, Ruby's Inn (☎ **435/834-5341**) sponsors several annual events, including the **Bryce Canyon Winter**

What Should I Take?

In packing for your trip, you'll want to be prepared for all your favorite activities, of course, but also keep in mind that this is a land of extremes, with an often-unforgiving climate and terrain. Those planning to hike or bike should take more drinking water containers than they think they'll need—experts recommend at least 1 gallon of water per person per day on the trail—as well as good-quality sunblock, hats and other protective clothing, and sunglasses with ultraviolet protection.

Summer visitors will want to carry rain gear for the typical afternoon thunderstorms, and jackets or sweaters for cool evenings. Winter visitors will not only want warm parkas and hats, but lighter clothing as well—the bright sun at midday, even in the high mountains of Bryce Canyon, can make it feel like June.

Take a first-aid kit, of course, and make sure it contains tweezers—very useful for removing cactus spines from your skin if you should make the mistake of getting too close. Hikers, especially those planning to go into the Narrows at Zion National Park, will appreciate having a walking stick to brace themselves against the sometimes strong currents on the "trail" that's actually more wading than hiking.

Festival in mid-February, a winter celebration with ski races, cross-country ski tours, and other activities.

Just outside Zion National Park, in Springdale, the **Western Heritage & Music Festival** (☎ **435/772-3757**) is held in mid-October, highlighting pioneer life with craft demonstrations, music, and food.

See chapter 8, "Gateway Towns," for additional information on nearby events.

IF YOU VISIT IN WINTER

Winter can be especially beautiful in both parks, and is definitely less crowded. Because there are fewer park visitors, rangers will have more time to answer questions and discuss the park's resources. In addition, you're likely to see more of the bigger animals, such as deer and elk, although some of the squirrels and reptiles will be hibernating, and many of the birds will have flown south seeking warmer climes (especially at Bryce).

There are disadvantages, of course. For one, far fewer ranger-led programs and activities are scheduled in winter. Also, sudden winter storms can keep you indoors and may leave hiking trails at both parks icy and treacherous. Those going to the parks in winter should carry a variety of clothing that can be worn in layers, to be added or subtracted as conditions change, and make sure to have warm boots with good traction soles. Because the roads getting to and from the parks are mountainous, cars should be equipped with snow tires and should have engine coolant that protects down to 20° below zero, just in case one of those rare cold fronts moves through.

3   Permits You Can Obtain in Advance

Permits for backcountry trips at both parks can be obtained several days in advance of the planned trip; however, they must be purchased in person at the visitor centers. Those planning to fish must first purchase state fishing licenses, which are available at sporting goods stores and other businesses throughout Utah. The basic rate for a non-resident 7-day fishing license is $17, plus a $6 Wildlife Habitat Authorization fee. For additional information contact the **Utah Division of Wildlife Resources,** 1596 W. North Temple, Salt Lake City, UT 84116 (☎ **877/592-5169** or 801/538-4700; www.nr.state.ut.us/dwr/!homeypg.htm), for the current *Utah Fishing Proclamation.* Zion National Park offers limited fishing opportunities; there are no bodies of water appropriate for fishing at Bryce Canyon National Park, although there is fishing nearby (see chapters 4 and 6 on hikes and other outdoor pursuits). Hunting is not permitted in either national park.

4   Getting There

Zion and Bryce Canyon National Parks are 83 miles apart by road.

GETTING TO ZION NATIONAL PARK

Zion National Park is located 46 miles northeast of St. George, 60 miles south of Cedar City, 83 miles southwest of Bryce Canyon National Park, and 120 miles northwest of the north rim of Grand Canyon National Park in northern Arizona. It's 309 miles south of Salt Lake City and 158 miles northeast of Las Vegas, Nevada.

BY CAR   From St. George travel north on I-15 10 miles to exit 16, then east on Utah 9 for 30 miles to the Zion Canyon section of the park. From Salt Lake City take I-15 south to exit 27, then Utah 17 south about 10 miles, and Utah 9 east about 20 miles. Though less scenic than the eastern approach to the park, this is the easiest route; it's more direct, avoids possible delays at the Zion–Mt. Carmel Tunnel, and delivers you to Springdale, just outside the park's southern entrance, where most of the area's lodging and restaurants are located. (See chapter 8, "Gateway Towns.")

The Kolob Canyons section, in the park's northwest corner, is reached via the short Kolob Canyons Road off I-15, exit 40.

From the east it's a spectacularly scenic 24-mile drive from Mt. Carmel Junction on Utah 9 (the Zion–Mt. Carmel Highway), reached from either the north or south via U.S. 89. However, be aware that this route into the park drops over 2,500 feet in elevation, passes through the mile-long Zion–Mt. Carmel Tunnel, and winds down six steep switchbacks. Oversized vehicles are charged $10 for use of the tunnel (see "Regulations" in chapter 3, "Exploring Zion National Park").

Bryce Canyon National Park is north and east of Mt. Carmel Junction via U.S. 89 north (44 miles) and Utah 12 east (13 miles). Kanab is 17 miles southeast of Mt. Carmel Junction along U.S. 89.

BY PLANE   There are small airports at St. George and Cedar City, both located along I-15, and from either it's easy to rent a car and drive to Zion. **Delta/Skywest Airlines** (☎ **800/453-9417** or 435/688-9508 in St. George, 435/586-3033 in Cedar City) flies into both airports.

Car rental agencies with St. George offices include **ABC** (☎ 435/628-7355); **Avis** (☎ 435/634-3940); **Budget** (☎ 435/673-6825); **Dollar** (☎ 435/628-6549); and **Quality** (☎ 435/634-0090). Car rental agencies at the Cedar City Airport include **National** (☎ 435/586-7059).

The closest major airport is **McCarran International Airport** in Las Vegas, Nevada (☎ **702/261-5211;** www.mccarran.com), which is about 120 miles southwest of St. George via I-15. Most major airlines fly into McCarran, and most major car rental agencies have outlets at the airport. The **St. George Shuttle** (☎ **800/933-8320** or 435/628-8320) provides daily service between St. George and the Las Vegas airport.

GETTING TO BRYCE CANYON NATIONAL PARK

Bryce Canyon National Park is 50 miles west of Escalante, 80 miles east of Cedar City, 83 miles northeast of Zion National Park, 120 miles southwest of Capitol Reef National Park, 135 miles northeast of St. George, and 160 miles north of the north rim of

Southern Utah Driving Times & Distances

Distances are given in miles. Times are estimated at a driving speed of 60 mph.

Grand Canyon National Park in northern Arizona. It's about 250 miles south of Salt Lake City.

BY CAR   From Zion National Park, head east on Utah 9 about 18 miles to U.S. 89, north 46 miles to Utah 12, and east 17 miles to the park entrance road (Utah 63). The Entrance Station is just 3 miles south of Utah 12.

From St. George travel north on I-15 10 miles to exit 16, east on Utah 9 for 63 miles to U.S. 89, north 44 miles to Utah 12, and east 17 miles to the park entrance road.

From Capitol Reef National Park, take Utah 24 west 10 miles to Torrey, turn southwest onto Scenic Highway Utah 12, through Boulder and Escalante, for about 110 miles to the park entrance road.

From Salt Lake City take I-15 south about 200 miles to exit 95, east 13 miles on Utah 20, south on U.S. 89 for 17 miles to Utah 12, and east 17 miles to the park entrance road.

BY PLANE   The closest airport with regularly scheduled flights is at Cedar City (see above).

Bryce Canyon Airport (☎ **435/834-5239**), at 7,586 feet elevation, is located several miles from the park entrance on Utah 12, and has a 7,400-foot lighted runway. Charter service is available from **Bryce Canyon Airlines** (☎ 435/834-5341). Car rentals at the airport are available from **Speedy** (☎ 435/834-5341) and **Bryce Canyon Car Rental** (☎ 800/432-5383 or 435/834-5200), which also has a desk in the lobby of Ruby's Inn.

5   Tips for RVers

One of the best ways to explore Zion and Bryce Canyon National Parks, especially in warmer months, is in an RV (a motor home, truck camper, or camper trailer) or in a car or truck while spending your nights in a tent—assuming you don't mind roughing it a bit.

One advantage to this type of travel is that early morning and early evening are among the best times to be in these parks, and it's a lot more convenient to experience the parks at these times if you're already there, staying in one of the park campgrounds. Another reason to camp is that if you have special dietary requirements, you won't have to worry about trying to find a restaurant that can meet your needs; you'll be able to cook for yourself, either in your RV or on a camp stove.

But the best reason is simply that inexplicable feeling of contentment that comes from waking up to the sound of birds singing and furry little creatures scurrying about outside your door; you're living the national park experience rather than just visiting as if it were an amusement park.

There are disadvantages, of course. Tents, small trailers, and campers can be cramped, and even the most luxurious motor homes and fifth-wheel trailers provide somewhat close quarters. Facilities in national park campgrounds are limited, although they are being upgraded to the point where camping purists are starting to complain. Even in most commercial campgrounds the facilities are less than you'd expect in moderately priced motels; and if you cook your own meals you miss the opportunity to experience the local cuisine. But, all this aside, camping is just plain fun—especially in settings as spectacular as Zion and Bryce Canyon.

There are a few things that RVers might want to know. Entering the park from the east in an RV will involve an extra fee and possibly a wait to get through the Zion–Mt. Carmel Tunnel, and there may be parking restrictions. However, you'll find that taking your RV into these parks isn't that much of a hassle, especially if you plan ahead.

For instance, parking is limited, especially for motor homes and other large vehicles, so take shuttle busses as much as possible, and drive either early or late in the day, when there's less traffic.

If you'll be traveling in the parks in your RV and want to make it obvious that your campsite is occupied, carry something worthless to leave in it, such as a cardboard box with "Site Taken" clearly written on it. You can usually find a rock to weight it down.

Because many of the national park campsites are not level, carry four or five short boards, or leveling blocks, that can be placed under the RV's wheels. You can buy small, inexpensive levels at RV and hardware stores, and you'll discover that not only will you sleep better if your rig is level, but your food won't slide off the table and the refrigerator will run more efficiently.

Once you've got an RV or tent, you'll need a place to put it, of course. Elsewhere in this book you'll find information on camping in Zion and Bryce Canyon National Parks, on nearby federal and state lands, and in the parks' gateway towns. Those planning to camp elsewhere in the state can get information on Utah's national forests from the **U.S. Forest Service,** Federal Building, Room 8103, 125 S. State St., Salt Lake City, UT 84138 (☎ **801/524-3900;** www.fs.fed.us/r4). The Utah State Office of the **U.S. Bureau of Land Management** is at 324 S. State St., Suite 301 (P.O. Box 45155), Salt Lake City, UT 84145-0155 (☎ **801/539-4001;** www.blm.gov/utah). For information on Utah's state parks, contact **Utah State Parks and Recreation,** 1594 W. North Temple, Suite 116 (P.O. Box 146001), Salt Lake City, UT 84114-6001 (☎ **801/ 538-7220,** 800/322-3770 for campground reservations; www.nr.state.ut.us/parks/utahstpk.htm).

There are 15 KOA franchise campgrounds in Utah. A nationwide directory is available free at any KOA, or by mail for $3 from **Kampgrounds of America (KOA), Inc.,** Executive Offices, Billings, MT 59114-0558. Their Web site is www.koa-kampgrounds.com. Members of the **American Automobile Association (AAA)** can request the club's free *Southwestern CampBook,* which includes campgrounds and RV parks in Utah, Arizona, Colorado, and New Mexico. And several massive campground directories can be purchased in major bookstores, including *Trailer Life Campground's, RV Parks, & Services* (www.tl.com) and *Woodall's Campground Directory* (www.woodalls.com).

Renting an RV for Your National Park Trek

If you own an RV, you're all set for a trip to Zion and Bryce Canyon National Parks; but if you don't, you might want to consider renting one. In fact, a study by two Canadian anthropologists has concluded that compared to the general population, those who travel in RVs are happier, healthier, and have a greater sense of community.

But first, let's get one thing straight: You probably won't save a lot of money. It is possible to travel fairly cheaply if you limit your equipment to a tent, a pop-up tent trailer, or a small pickup truck camper—but renting a motor home will probably end up costing almost as much as driving a compact car, staying in moderately priced motels, and eating in family-style restaurants and cafes. That's because the motor home will go only one-third as far on a gallon of gas as your compact car, and they're expensive to rent (generally between $1,000 and $1,100 per week in mid-summer, when rates are highest).

But carrying your house with you, like a turtle, gives you the opportunity to stay in the national park campgrounds, which many park visitors believe is one of the highlights of their trip. It also lets you stop for meals anytime and anywhere you choose; and it means you won't have to worry about sleeping on a lumpy pillow. An added benefit is that you won't spend time searching for a rest room—almost all RVs have some sort of bathroom facilities, ranging from a full bath with tub/shower combo to a porta-potty stored under a seat.

If you're planning to fly into the area and rent an RV when you arrive, choose your starting point carefully. Not only will you want to keep the driving to a minimum, but rental rates vary, depending on the city in which you pick up your RV. Rental rates are usually less in Las Vegas, Nevada than in Salt Lake City, and since most of Utah's national parks are closer to Las Vegas than Salt Lake City anyway, you could save by starting and ending your trip in Las Vegas.

The country's largest RV rental company, with outlets in Las Vegas and Salt Lake City, is **Cruise America** (☎ **800/327-7799;** fax 602/464-7321; www.cruiseamerica.com). RV rentals are also available from **El Monte RV** (☎ **800/367-3687** or 562/483-4941; www.elmonte.com), with rental locations in California, Washington, Florida, and New Jersey. Information on additional rental agencies, as well as tips on renting, can be obtained from the **Recreation Vehicle Rental Association,** 3930 University Dr., Fairfax, VA 22030 (www.rvra.org).

6 Adventure Vacations & Organized Tours

A number of nationally recognized organizations offer tours and other activities that include the Zion and Bryce Canyon National Park areas. In most cases, all you do is pay your money and they arrange everything, including lodging, meals, and transportation. These range from fairly standard bus tours to adventure vacations where you spend your days hiking or biking, but are pampered with gourmet meals, hot tubs, and first-class hotels at night. You'll want to contact these operators as far in advance as possible, since reservations are required, and group sizes are limited. The adventure tour operators generally specialize in small groups and have trips for various levels of ability and physical condition. Trips are offered in a range of price categories, from basic to luxurious, and are of varying lengths.

American Orient Express Railway Company, 2025 First Ave., Suite 830, Seattle, WA 98121 (☎ **888/759-3944** or 206/441-2725; www.americanorientexpress.com), offers a luxurious excursion that includes side trips to Zion and Bryce Canyon National Parks. You'll travel in trains with restored vintage passenger cars outfitted in polished mahogany and brass, and dining cars decked out with china, silver, crystal, and linen, and a cuisine to match.

American Wilderness Experience, 2820-A Wilderness Place, P.O. Box 1486, Boulder, CO 80306 (☎ **800/444-0099** or 303/444-2622; fax 303/444-3999; www.awetrips.com), offers mountain biking, hiking, horseback riding, and other adventure vacations, including multiday trips in the Grand Staircase–Escalante National Monument area, just east of Bryce Canyon National Park.

Backcountry Vacations, P.O. Box 4029, Bozeman, MT 59772 (☎ **800/575-1540** or 406/586-3556; fax 406/586-4288; www.backcountrytours.com), provides guided multiday mountain biking, hiking, and combination tours in the Bryce Canyon and Zion national parks areas.

Backroads, 801 Cedar St., Berkeley, CA 94710-1800 (☎ **800/462-2848** or 510/527-1555; fax 510/527-1444; www.backroads.com), offers a variety of multiday guided biking and hiking tours to the national parks in southern Utah. There's a road-bike tour to Zion, Bryce, and the Grand Canyon; and hiking tours of the Zion and Bryce areas.

Gray Line Motor Tours, 553 W. 100 S., Salt Lake City, UT 84101 (☎ **800/309-2352** or 801/521-7060; www.grayline.com), offers several national park bus tour packages in the summer, including a 3-day, 2-night trip to Zion, Bryce Canyon, and Grand Canyon National Parks.

Maupintour, 1515 St. Andrews Dr., Lawrence, KS 66047 (☎ **800/255-4266** or 913/843-1211), one of the world's largest tour companies, offers guided trips to the state's national parks, including Zion and Bryce Canyon.

Roads Less Traveled, 2840 Wilderness Place, #F, Boulder, CO 80301 (☎ **800/488-8483** or 303/413-0938; fax 303/413-0926; www.roadslesstraveled.com), offers backcountry hiking and biking tours throughout the Southwest, including Bryce and Zion.

Tauck Tours, 276 Post Rd. W., P.O. Box 5027, Westport, CT 06881-5027 (☎ **800/468-2825** or 203/226-6911), offers a variety of tours, including one that includes Zion and Bryce Canyon National Parks.

7 Tips for Travelers with Disabilities

Both Zion and Bryce Canyon National Parks have made great strides in the past few years in making their facilities more accessible to those with disabilities. Visitor centers at both parks are wheelchair accessible, including the rest rooms. At Bryce Canyon, a half-mile section of the Rim Trail, between Sunrise and Sunset Points, is fairly level, paved, and wheelchair accessible; several of the viewpoints along the scenic drive are accessible; the Bristlecone Loop Trail at Rainbow Point has a hard surface and is accessible with assistance; and Sunset Campground has accessible campsites. In Zion, accessible campsites are available in South Campground; Riverside Walk at the end of Zion Canyon Scenic Drive is paved and accessible with assistance; Pa'rus Trail is a 2-mile paved and accessible trail, open also to bicyclists. In addition, rangers at both parks are extremely receptive to helping visitors with disabilities to get the most out of their national park visits.

The National Park Service's **Golden Access Passport,** available free at all national parks, is a lifetime pass that is issued to any U.S. citizen or permanent resident who is medically certified as disabled or blind. The pass permits free entry and gives a 50% discount on park service campgrounds and activities, but it does not cover user fees or charges for services offered by private concessionaires.

The Utah information and referral line for people with disabilities is ☎ 800/333-8824.

Amtrak will, with 24 hours' notice, provide porter service, special seating, and a discount (☎ **800/USA-RAIL**). If you're traveling with a companion, **Greyhound** will carry you both for a single fare (☎ **800/231-2222**). Both Amtrak and Greyhound have scheduled stops in St. George and Cedar City.

Many of the major car rental companies now offer hand-controlled cars for disabled drivers. **Avis** can provide such a vehicle at any of its locations in the U.S. with 48-hour advance notice; **Hertz** requires between 24 and 72 hours of advance reservation at most of its locations. **Wheelchair Getaways** (☎ **800/873-4973;** www.blvd.com/wg.htm) rents specialized vans with wheelchair lifts and other features for the disabled in more than 100 cities across the United States.

8 Tips for Travelers with Pets

National parks, including Zion and Bryce Canyon, as well as other federal lands administered by the National Park Service, are not pet-friendly, and those planning to visit the parks should consider leaving their pets at home. Pets are prohibited on all hiking trails, in the backcountry, and in all buildings, and must always be on a leash no more than 6 feet long. Pets also should not be left unattended in campgrounds at either park. Essentially, this means that if you take your pet into the parks they can be with you in the campgrounds and inside your vehicle, and you can walk them in parking areas, but that's about it. It's no fun for either you or your pet.

Aside from regulations, though, you need to be concerned with your pet's well being. Pets should never be left in closed vehicles, where temperatures can soar to over 120°F in minutes, resulting in brain damage or death, and there is no punishment too severe for the human who subjects a dog or cat to that torture. At this writing, there are no boarding kennels within 80 miles of Bryce Canyon National Park. Pet boarding is available in several communities near Zion; contact the **park office** (☎ **435/772-3256**) for current information.

Special Tip for Pet Owners

Although pets are not permitted on the trails or backcountry in Bryce Canyon and Zion National Parks, those traveling with their dogs can hike with them over miles of trails administered by the U.S. Forest Service and Bureau of Land Management, adjacent to both national parks. Pets are also welcome, even on trails, in Grand Staircase–Escalante National Monument (administered by the BLM) and in Utah's state parks (see chapter 9, "Nearby Things to See & Do").

Those who do decide to take pets with them into these parks despite the above warnings should take the pets' leashes (of course); carry plenty of water (pet shops sell clever little travel water bowls that won't spill in a moving vehicle); and proof that the dogs or cats have been vaccinated against rabies. Flea and tick spray or powder is also important, especially if you will be taking your pet to Bryce Canyon, where bubonic plague is transmitted by the fleas of prairie dogs and other rodents (see chapter 5, "Exploring Bryce Canyon National Park").

9 Tips for Travelers with Children

Visiting Zion and Bryce Canyon National Parks with your children can be an especially rewarding experience, and is an excellent way for everyone—children and adults alike—to learn about the parks' geology, plants, and animals, as well as to appreciate the unequaled beauty of nature.

However, these parks are in relatively remote areas, and their gateway cities are little more than small towns. There are no major chain grocery or discount stores, and although you will be able to buy items such as baby food and disposable diapers, you may not find the brands or types that you're used to. Most parents carry a good supply of these items with them, or stock up before they leave larger communities such as Salt Lake City or St. George. It's also a good idea to carry any prescription drugs you might want, and also to make sure you have the phone numbers of your doctor and pharmacist.

10 Protecting Your Health & Safety

The rugged landscapes that make Zion and Bryce Canyon such beautiful destinations can also be hazardous to your health, especially if you're not used to their extremes of climate and altitude. Since the isolation of many of the areas you'll seek out means there may be no one there to help in an emergency, the answer is to be prepared, like any good Boy Scout (see box entitled "What Should I Take?," earlier in this chapter). Most importantly, before heading out check with park offices, park rangers, and other local outdoor specialists about current conditions.

Southern Utah's extremes of **climate**—from burning desert to snow-covered mountains—can produce health problems if you're not prepared. If you haven't been to the desert before, it can be

Warning: Parking Lot

Over half the traffic accidents at Bryce Canyon National Park occur in the parking lots.

difficult to comprehend the heat, dryness, and intensity of the sun. If you're prone to dry skin, moisturizing lotion is a must; even if you're not, you will probably end up using it. Everyone needs to use a good quality sunblock, wear a hat, and wear sunglasses with full ultraviolet protection. Hikers and others planning to be outside will also need to carry water—at least a gallon per person per day is recommended.

The other potential problem is **elevation.** Bryce Canyon National Park rises to over 9,000 feet, and a side trip to Cedar Breaks National Monument (see chapter 9, "Nearby Things to See & Do") will take you to over 10,000 feet. Although not as high as some of Utah's mountains, which soar to over 13,000 feet, the upper elevations here are still high enough to produce health problems for those not accustomed to them. The problem is, there's less oxygen and lower humidity up there than many visitors are used to. In fact, the most common complaint at the first-aid station at Bryce Canyon Lodge is shortness of breath. Those with heart or respiratory problems should consult their doctors before planning a trip to these parks, Bryce Canyon in particular. If you're in generally good health, you don't need to take any special precautions, but it's advisable to ease into high elevations by changing altitude gradually. Also, get plenty of rest, avoid large meals, and drink plenty of nonalcoholic fluids, especially water.

State health officials also warn outdoor enthusiasts to take precautions against the **Hantavirus,** a rare but often fatal respiratory disease, first recognized in 1993. About half of the country's confirmed cases have been reported in the Four Corners states of Colorado, New Mexico, Arizona, and Utah. The disease is usually spread by the urine and droppings of rodents, and health officials recommend that campers and hikers avoid areas with signs of rodent occupation. Symptoms of Hantavirus are similar to flu, and lead to breathing difficulties and shock.

Other park-specific problems are bubonic plague, which is discussed in chapter 5, "Exploring Bryce Canyon National Park," and flash flooding, which is discussed in chapter 4, "Hikes & Other Outdoor Pursuits in Zion National Park."

11   Protecting the Environment

Many of the wonderful outdoor areas you'll be exploring in Zion and Bryce Canyon National Parks are quite isolated, especially in the backcountry at Zion. Although you're certainly not the first human being to set foot there, you may feel like you are. Not long ago, the rule of thumb was to "leave only footprints"; these days, we're trying to do better and not leave even footprints. It's relatively easy to be a good outdoor citizen—mostly common sense. Pack out all trash, stay on established trails, be especially careful not to pollute water, and, in general, do your best to have as little impact on the environment as possible. Some hikers go further, carrying a small trash bag to pick up what others may have left. As the park service likes to remind us, protecting our national parks is everyone's responsibility.

3

Exploring Zion National Park

*U*tah's most popular national park, Zion is a spectacularly beautiful spot, where you'll discover a wide variety of sights and experiences. Here you'll see the minute Zion snail—almost too small to see at all—and a variety of birds and other creatures of practically all shapes and sizes. There are massive rock formations, such as the Great White Throne, that give one the feeling that this is something permanent—solid as a rock, as the saying goes—but we can also experience the beautiful Narrows, and the evidence of how time and water have carved huge chunks of stone into a delicate work of art, and how that sculpting continues today.

1 Essentials

ACCESS/ENTRY POINTS   Located in southwest Utah, Zion National Park has two main sections: **Zion Canyon,** the main part of the park, where everyone goes; and the less-visited **Kolob Canyons.** The main east-west road through Zion Canyon is the park-owned extension of Utah 9; from here the park's 14-mile round-trip Zion Canyon Road heads north, providing access to most scenic overlooks and trailheads.

Utah 9 crosses Zion National Park, giving the main section of the park two entry gates—south and east. The south entrance, at Springdale, is by far the more popular, with two-thirds of park visitors arriving there. Most area lodging and restaurants are found in Springdale (see chapter 8, "Gateway Towns"). In addition, the park's two campgrounds and the Zion Canyon Visitor Center are located just inside the south entrance.

There is no town at the east gateway, but that route is more scenic—it drops over 2,500 feet in elevation, passes through the mile-long Zion–Mt. Carmel Tunnel, and winds down six steep switchbacks. The tunnel is too small for two-way traffic that includes vehicles larger than standard passenger cars and pickup trucks, so oncoming traffic must be stopped to let them through (see "Regulations," below). Those visiting Bryce Canyon National Park will probably enter or leave Zion through the east entrance.

Zion National Park

39

Where to Find Rest Rooms in Zion

The all-important rest rooms at Zion are generally well maintained, but vary considerably in the facilities offered. As at most national parks, the best are at the visitor centers, where you'll find heated rooms with flush toilets and sinks. There are also public rest rooms at the Zion Lodge shuttle stop. South and Watchman Campgrounds, the Grotto Picnic Area, and the Temple of Sinawava Trailhead have flush toilets and sinks. Lava Point Campground, Kolob Canyons Viewpoint, and Weeping Rock and Canyon Overlook Trailheads have vault toilets. Although essentially outhouses, this type of facility has come a long way in the past 20 years—they're clean, sanitary, and best of all they don't smell. However, there are no lights, no water for hand washing, and no heat. There are no toilets along trails or in the backcountry.

During busy times, the campground, picnic area, and trailhead facilities may run out of toilet paper, so it's best to carry a backup source.

The **Kolob Canyons** section, in the park's northwest corner, is easily reached on the short Kolob Canyons Road off I-15, at exit 40.

About 15 miles west of Zion Canyon, Kolob Terrace Road heads north from the village of Virgin off Utah 9, providing access to several backcountry trails (see chapter 4, "Hikes & Other Outdoor Pursuits in Zion National Park") and the Lava Point Campground (see chapter 7, "Where to Stay & Eat in the Parks"). This road is closed in the winter.

To get to Bryce Canyon National Park, head north and east on Utah 9, U.S. 89, and Utah 12.

VISITOR CENTERS & INFORMATION   The park has two visitor centers. The **Zion Canyon Visitor Center & Transportation Hub** (☎ 435/772-3256), near the south entrance to the park, was scheduled to open in summer 2000, with a wide variety of outdoor exhibits. Rangers answer questions and provide backcountry permits, free brochures are available, and books, maps, videos, postcards, and posters are sold. The **Kolob Canyons Visitor Center** (☎ 435/586-9548), in the northwest corner of the park off I-15, provides information, permits, books, and maps. Both visitor centers are open 8am to 7pm in summer, with shorter hours the rest of the year.

FEES   Entry into the park (for up to 7 days), which includes unlimited use of the shuttle bus, costs $20 per private vehicle, $5 per individual on motorcycle or bicycle, or $4 per individual for those on foot using the pedestrian-only entrance. Golden Eagle, Golden Access, and Golden Age passes are honored. Oversized vehicles (see "Regulations," below) are charged $10 for use of the Zion–Mt. Carmel Tunnel on the east side of the park.

Permits, available at either visitor center, are required for all overnight trips into the backcountry. Cost is $5 per person per night. Camping costs $10 per night for basic campsites and $14 per night for sites with electric hookups (located in Watchman Campground).

REGULATIONS   The mile-long Zion–Mt. Carmel Tunnel (see "Historic & Man-Made Attractions," below) is too small for two-way traffic that includes vehicles larger than standard passenger cars and pickup trucks. Buses, trucks, and most recreational vehicles must be driven down the center of the tunnel, and therefore all oncoming traffic must be stopped. This applies to all vehicles over 7'10" wide (including mirrors) or 11'4" tall (including luggage racks and so forth). For affected vehicles, there is a $10 fee, good for two trips through the tunnel during a 7-day period, which is paid at the entrance stations. Hours for escorts are limited during winter months (get details at park entrances or by calling park headquarters). All vehicles over 13'1" tall and certain other particularly large vehicles are prohibited from driving anywhere on the park road between the east entrance and Zion Canyon.

Bicycles are prohibited in the Zion–Mt. Carmel Tunnel, the backcountry, and on trails, except the Pa'rus Trail. Feeding or molesting wildlife, vandalism, and disturbing any natural feature of the park is forbidden. Dogs, which must be leashed at all times, are prohibited on all trails, in the backcountry, and in public buildings.

Backcountry hikers should practice minimum impact techniques and are prohibited from building fires. A new general management plan was being prepared that will set limits for the number of people allowed in various parts of the backcountry; prospective backcountry hikers should check with rangers before setting out. A free booklet on backcountry travel, available at the visitor centers, lists all regulations plus descriptions of close to 20 backcountry trails.

FAST FACTS

ATMs　The closest automated teller machine (ATM) to the park is at the **Zion Canyon Theatre Complex** (☎ 435/772-2400), just outside the south entrance, at 145 Zion Park Blvd. There is also an ATM at **Zions Bank,** 921 Zion Park Blvd. (☎ 435/772-3274).

Car Trouble/Towing Services　Emergency 24-hour service is available from **W. J. Bassett Repair** (☎ 435/772-3328) in Springdale for autos, buses, motor homes, etc.

Emergencies　Dial ☎ 911 or 435/772-3322 24 hours a day, or locate the nearest park ranger.

Gas Stations　**Springdale Chevron** is located on the south side of town at 1593 Zion Park Blvd. (☎ 435/772-3922). Just outside the east entrance to the park there is a gas station.

Laundry　There are no laundry facilities in Zion National Park, but coin-operated laundries are located at **Zion Canyon Campground** (☎ 435/772-3237), just outside the park's east entrance, and in downtown Springdale in the **Zion Park Motel** complex (☎ 435/772-3251). Just outside the park's east entrance, there is a coin-operated laundry at **Mukuntuweep RV Park & Campground** (☎ 435/648-2154).

Medical Services　The **Zion Medical Clinic,** 120 Lion Blvd., Springdale (☎ 435/772-3226) is open daily from May through October, and about 1 day a week the rest of the year. For medical emergencies, dial ☎ 911 or 435/772-3322 24 hours a day, or locate the nearest park ranger. One of the larger hospitals in this part of the state is **Dixie Regional Medical Center,** 544 S. 400 E., St. George (☎ 435/634-4000). From the east entrance, the nearest medical facility is the **Kane County Hospital & Skilled Nursing Facility,** 220 W. 300 N. St., Kanab (☎ 435/644-5811).

Permits　Permits, available at the visitor centers, are required for overnight backcountry camping (see "Fees," under "Essentials," above), and special permits are also necessary to drive RVs and other large vehicles through the Zion–Mt. Carmel Tunnel (see "Regulations," under "Essentials," above).

Post Offices　There is a post office inside Zion Lodge (ZIP 84767) and mail drops at each of the visitor centers. Springdale's post office (ZIP 84767) is located at 624 Zion Park Blvd. (☎ 800/275-8777 for hours and other post office locations).

Supplies   You'll find most of the groceries and camping and RV supplies you want in Springdale, just outside the park's south entrance. At **Zion Canyon Campground,** on Zion Park Boulevard a half mile south of the park's south entrance (☎ **435/772-3237**), is a store with groceries, souvenirs, and RV supplies, plus a restaurant. In downtown Springdale, the **Zion Park Market,** 855 Zion Park Blvd. (☎ **435/772-3251**), stocks a good selection of groceries, plus has video rentals. On the south end of Springdale on Utah 9 (the opposite side of town from the national park), is the highly recommended **Springdale Fruit Company** (☎ **435/772-3222**), which sells fresh organic fruits, vegetables, and juices (try the fruit smoothies), plus trail mix and baked goods. It also has a picnic area. The **Switchback C-Store,** 1149 S. Zion Park Blvd. (☎ **435/772-3700**) stocks snacks and pastries and contains the local **state liquor store.** Those in need of outdoor equipment, hiking boots, clothing, and the like will find what they need at **Zion Outdoor,** 868 Zion Park Blvd. (☎ **435/772-0630**).

Just outside the east entrance to the park, there is a small store, gas station, restaurant, curio shop, and campground.

Telephones   Public telephones are located at the visitor center, Zion Lodge, and both Watchman and South campgrounds.

Weather   For current statewide weather information, contact the **National Weather Service** (☎ **801/524-5133;** http://nimbo. wrh.noaa.gov/saltlake). For local weather information, call the park office at ☎ **435/772-3256,** Monday to Friday from 8am to 4:30pm.

2 Tips from a Park Ranger

"Overpowering, but also intimate" is how former backcountry Ranger Dave Rachlis sees Zion National Park, adding, "These are some of the highest vertical rock walls that some people will ever see."

An added bonus is an extensive and highly accessible trail system, much of which was constructed in the 1920s and 1930s. "The park has a sense of grandeur, but then it also has access," says Rachlis. "You can go up the West Rim Trail or you can go up the East Rim Trail, and you can get into these narrow canyons, and really experience the park pretty easily."

Rachlis says that most visitors to Zion see only a small part of the park—what's visible from the viewpoints—but he recommends that visitors stay at least a full day, adding, "In 2 or 3 days, you can see most of the major regions of the park, and get a chance to get out on the trails a bit for day hikes." Those who want to explore the backcountry will need more time.

A hike through the Narrows is "the ultimate slot canyon experience," says Rachlis. "You're following a drainage, wading or swimming in a river in spots—in summer it's one of the cooler areas of the park." He adds, "One of the unique aspects of the Narrows is that the river runs year-round."

Rachlis also recommends the relatively easy La Verkin Creek Trail, which leads to Kolob Arch, believed to be the world's largest freestanding arch. "It's very intimate, very colorful—the rock is a little more orange-to-red than it is in the main canyon." For the best scenery, Rachlis directs people to the West Rim Trail, which gets you up onto the plateau where you can look down into the canyons.

One mistake some park visitors make, Rachlis says, is to downplay the dangers of the easy and moderate hiking trails, where most injuries occur. He says that people understand the hazards on difficult trails such as Angels Landing, where you're inching along a knife-edge ridge; but you also need to be careful on trails with less-obvious dangers. "Sandstone is slippery, and a 20-foot fall can kill you as easily as a 1,000-foot fall."

Zion National Park has a growing reputation as a destination for rock climbers, but Rachlis says this is not the place for beginners. "There are no bolts placed on the walls for the most part; it's free climbing, where people put their own anchoring in and then pull it out as they go up. Because of the softness of the rock, the difficulty of the crack systems here, it's not recommended for casual climbers—it's an expert climber's paradise." He recommends that those with less than expert rock climbing skills go to Snow Canyon State Park (see chapter 9, "Nearby Things to See & Do").

As for when to visit, Rachlis says the trails can be hot in summer, so the best time for hiking is probably spring and fall—from April to June and from September to November. The park is also less crowded then. But he adds that the park has unpredictable weather, so it's best to call to check on current conditions before showing up ready to hike.

3 The Highlights

There is such a wide variety of things to do and see here that it's difficult to say which are the highlights, but probably the single most important activity for visitors is traveling the ✪ **Zion Canyon Road** on the shuttle bus, getting off at viewpoints where you can see many of the park's best-known rock formations.

Among the spectacular rock formations you won't want to miss is ✪ **the Great White Throne,** which can be seen from Zion Canyon Road as well as from several hiking trails, including Observation Point Trail, Deertrap Mountain Trail, Angels Landing Trail, and Emerald Pools Trail (see chapter 4, "Hikes & Other Outdoor Pursuits in Zion National Park"). Considered the symbol of Zion National Park for many visitors, this massive and imposing block of Navajo sandstone towers 2,000 feet above the North Fork of the Virgin River. It can be especially impressive when colored by the setting sun. A postage stamp depicting the Great White Throne was issued in the 1930s.

Another eye-catcher is the huge **Checkerboard Mesa,** which you pass when entering the park from the east. Looking as though it was etched by some giant hand, this huge dome of sandstone has a fishnet pattern created by a unique form of erosion and weathering. Although horizontal lines in Navajo sandstone are fairly common, the rare vertical lines are believed to have been formed by freezing and thawing processes, and then enlarged by running water. For more see "Seeing the Park by Car and Shuttle," below.

Those who think of southern Utah as nothing but burning desert will learn differently at **Weeping Rock,** a short but steep walk along Weeping Rock Trail. Its name derives from the fact that water continually runs down the vertical face of the rock, nurturing hanging gardens. For more, see chapter 4, "Hikes & Other Outdoor Pursuits in Zion National Park," and chapter 10, "A Nature Guide to Zion & Bryce Canyon National Parks."

The **Emerald Pools** provide another look at the wet side of Zion—lush green plants, pretty pools of water, and two delightful cascading waterfalls. Located in a short canyon near Zion Lodge, the lower pool is an easy walk along a paved path, while the two upper pools require a bit of real hiking. The pools are named for their rich green color, the result of algae in the water. You'll find more information in chapter 4, "Hikes & Other Outdoor Pursuits in Zion National Park."

At the end of the Zion Canyon Road is the **Temple of Sinawava,** a picturesque canyon surrounded by rock walls reaching 2,000 feet

---

Photo Tip

The key to getting good wildlife photos is to know the animals' habits, such as where they go and when. Then, get there first and quietly wait.

Zion Canyon

into the sky. Here, you'll discover the aptly named Pulpit and Altar rock formations, as well as maple and cottonwood trees and a spectacular seasonal waterfall that cascades almost 1,000 feet down the temple's west wall. This is the beginning of the Riverside Walk, discussed below and in chapter 4, "Hikes & Other Outdoor Pursuits in Zion National Park."

The **Riverside Walk,** considered the park's easiest trail, should not be ignored just because it's not a challenge. It begins at the Temple of Sinawava and parallels the Virgin River, providing a good sense of the steepness of the canyon walls as you approach the Narrows. Along the walk are interpretive signs discussing this particular ecosystem, and this is a good place to hear and possibly see, the canyon tree frog, plus the American dipper and other park wildlife. For additional information, see chapter 4, "Hikes & Other Outdoor Pursuits in Zion National Park," and chapter 10, "A Nature Guide to Zion & Bryce Canyon National Parks."

For a unique hiking experience as well as a close-up look at the power of water, you'll want to venture into **the Narrows,** a section of the Virgin River where the canyon walls are less than 30 feet in spots but stand over 1,000 feet tall. To travel between these delicately sculpted rock walls, you'll hike and wade. The Narrows can be experienced as a short day hike, a long 1-day-through hike, or an overnight hike—although caution is needed because the Narrows is prone to flash flooding. For details, see chapter 4, "Hikes & Other Outdoor Pursuits in Zion National Park" and chapter 10, "A Nature Guide to Zion & Bryce Canyon National Parks."

An often-overlooked area of Zion National Park is the **Kolob Canyons** section, in the park's northwest corner. With its narrow canyons and brightly colored cliffs, this is a somewhat different world than Zion Canyon. There's a scenic drive with spectacular overlooks, and several hiking trails. See the section "Seeing the Park by Car and Shuttle," below, as well as chapter 4, "Hikes & Other Outdoor Pursuits in Zion National Park."

Wildlife Viewing & Bird Watching

It's a rare visitor to Zion who doesn't spot a critter of some sort, from **mule deer**—often observed along roadways and in campgrounds year-round—to the numerous varieties of lizards seen from spring through fall, including the park's largest lizard, the **chuckwalla,** which can grow to 20 inches. There has been an increasing number of sightings of **desert bighorn sheep** and even an occasional **mountain lion** along Utah 9 (the Zion–Mt. Carmel Highway) on the east side of the park. Along the Virgin River, you'll see **bank beaver,** so named because they live in burrows dug into riverbanks instead of building dams.

If you're interested in spotting birds, you're in luck at Zion. The **peregrine falcon,** among the world's fastest birds, is sometimes seen along the Angels Landing and Cable Mountain trails and in the area of the Great White Throne. It sometimes nests in the Weeping Rock area, where you're also likely to see the American dipper, canyon wren, and white-throated swift. **Bald eagles** sometimes winter in the park; and you might also see golden eagles. **Red-tailed hawks** are fairly common, plus you're likely to see great blue herons, American kestrels, Gambel's quail, mourning doves, great horned owls, western kingbirds, common ravens, piñon jays, Steller's jays, yellow-rumped warblers, and American robins.

Snakes include the poisonous **Great Basin rattlesnake,** found below 8,000 feet elevation; there are also nonpoisonous king snakes and gopher snakes. Amphibians found in the park include the Arizona tiger salamander, Great Basin spadefoot, red-spotted toad, and northern leopard frog. **Tarantulas,** those large, usually slow-moving hairy spiders, are often seen in late summer and fall. Contrary to popular belief, the tarantula's bite is not significantly poisonous to most people, although it may be somewhat painful.

Remember, it's illegal to feed the wildlife. No matter how much you may want to befriend an animal by offering food, please remember that it's not healthy for the wildlife to eat human food or to get used to being fed this way. For additional details on the wildlife at Zion, see chapter 10, "A Nature Guide to Zion & Bryce Canyon National Parks."

4   How to See the Park in 1 or 2 Days

The best way to see Zion is to spend a week, starting with the visitor center displays and programs, then a Zion Canyon Road trip on the shuttle bus, and gradually working from short hikes and walks to full-day and overnight treks into the backcountry. That's the ideal; but for most visitors, time and finances dictate a shorter visit.

If you have only a day or two, we recommend that your first stop be the **Zion Canyon Visitor Center** to see the exhibits, look through the free *Zion Park Map & Guide,* which describes the available options, and finally talk with a ranger about the amount of time you have, your abilities, and interests. Because Zion has such a variety of landscapes and activities, each visitor can easily create his own itinerary.

If your goal is to see as much of the park as possible in 1 full day, we suggest the following:

After a quick stop at the visitor center, hop on the shuttle bus, which hits the major Zion Canyon roadside viewpoints. But, when you get to the **Temple of Sinawava,** instead of just taking a quick look and jumping on the next shuttle, hike the easy 2-mile round-trip **Riverside Walk,** which follows the Virgin River through a narrow canyon past hanging gardens. Then continue the shuttle bus trek back to the lodge (total time: 2 to 4 hours), where you might stop at the gift shop and possibly have lunch in the lodge restaurant.

Near the lodge, you'll find the trailhead for the **Emerald Pools.** Especially pleasant on hot days, this easy walk through a forest of oak, maple, fir, and cottonwood trees leads to a waterfall, hanging garden, and the shimmering lower pool. This part of the walk should take about an hour round-trip; but those with a bit more ambition may want to add another hour and another mile to the loop by taking the moderately strenuous hike on a rocky, steeper trail to the upper pool.

If you still have time and energy, drive back toward the south park entrance and stop at **Watchman Trailhead.** Here, a moderately strenuous, 2-mile, 2-hour round-trip hike takes you to a plateau with beautiful views of several rock formations and the town of Springdale. For details on these trails, see chapter 4, "Hikes & Other Outdoor Pursuits in Zion National Park." That evening, try to take in the campground amphitheater program.

5 Seeing the Park by Car & Shuttle

If you enter the park from the east, along the steep **Zion–Mt. Carmel Highway,** you'll travel 13 miles to the **Zion Canyon Visitor Center,** passing between the White Cliffs and Checkerboard Mesa, a massive sandstone rock formation covered with horizontal and vertical lines that make it look like a huge fishing net. Continuing, you'll pass through a fairyland of fantastically shaped rocks of red, orange, tan, and white, as well as the **Great Arch of Zion,** carved by the forces of erosion high in a stone cliff. At the east end of the Zion–Mt. Carmel Tunnel is the **trailhead parking** for the Canyon Overlook Trail, a relatively easy 1-mile walk to a great viewpoint (see chapter 4, "Hikes & Other Outdoor Pursuits in Zion National Park"). After driving through the tunnel (see "Regulations," under "Essentials," above), you'll traverse a number of long switchbacks as you descend to the canyon floor.

A shuttle bus system, scheduled to begin in spring 2000, has been implemented in the main section of the park to reduce traffic congestion and the resultant problems of pollution, noise, and damage to park resources. The shuttle system consists of two loops: one in the town of Springdale and the other along Zion Canyon Road, with the loops connecting at the new transit/visitor center just inside the south park entrance (see above). From March through October, access to Zion Canyon Road (above Utah 9) will be limited to shuttle busses, hikers, and bikers. The only exception will be overnight Zion Lodge guests and tour busses connected with the lodge, who will have access as far as the lodge. Shuttle stops are located at all the major-use areas in the park, and shuttles will run frequently (about every 6 minutes at peak times). In winter, when visitation is lowest in the park, visitors will be permitted to drive the full length of Zion Canyon Road in their own vehicles. Complete information about the shuttle and all stops is available at the new visitor center.

The ride through Zion Canyon is impressive by any standards, with massive stone reaching straight up to the heavens, and the North Fork of the Virgin River threading its way through the maze of rocks. In every direction the views are awe-inspiring. Pullouts

Factoid

The Navajo sandstone that forms Zion's rock walls is one of the thickest sedimentary formations in the world—2,200 feet at its thickest point, which is in the West Temple formation.

Wildlife Viewing Tip

The earlier in the day you can get out on the Zion Canyon Road, the better chance you'll have of seeing wildlife.

along the road provide access to viewpoints and hiking trails (see chapter 4, "Hikes & Other Outdoor Pursuits in Zion National Park").

The first pullout is across from the **Court of the Patriarchs,** where a short paved trail leads to an impressive viewpoint. The next stop is **Zion Lodge** (see chapter 7, "Where to Stay & Eat in the Parks"), and across the road from the lodge is the trailhead for the **Emerald Pools trail system.** The Grotto Picnic Area is about a half mile beyond the lodge, and a trail, paralleling Zion Canyon Road, leads from the lodge to the picnic area. Across from the Grotto Picnic Area parking lot is a footbridge that leads to the Emerald Pools, Angels Landing, and West Rim trails.

Continuing north into Zion Canyon, the road passes the **Great White Throne** on the right and then **Angels Landing** on the left, before the turnoff to the **Weeping Rock Trailhead** parking area. From here the road closely traces the curves of the river, with a couple of stops to allow different views of **the Organ,** which to some resembles a huge pipe organ. Finally the road ends at the **Temple of Sinawava,** where the paved **Riverside Walk** follows the Virgin River toward **the Narrows,** one of the most incredible sights in Zion.

To escape the crowds of Zion Canyon, head to the northwest corner of the park. The **Kolob Canyons Road** (about 45 minutes from Zion Canyon Visitor Center at I-15 exit 40) runs 5 miles among spectacular red and orange rocks, ending at a high vista. Allow about 45-minutes round-trip, including stopping at numbered viewpoints. Be sure to get a copy of the Kolob Canyons Road Guide at the Kolob Visitor Center. Here's what you'll pass along the way:

Leaving **Kolob Canyons Visitor Center,** you'll drive along the Hurricane Fault to **Hurricane Cliffs,** a series of tall, gray cliffs composed of limestone, and onward to **Taylor Creek,** where a piñon-juniper forest clings to life on the rocky hillside, providing a home to the bright blue scrub jay. Your next stop is **Horse Ranch Mountain,** which, at 8,726 feet, is the national park's highest point. Passing a series of colorful rock layers, where you might be lucky enough to spot a golden eagle, your next stop is **Box Canyon,** along the South Fork of Taylor Creek, with sheer rock walls soaring over

1,500 feet high. Along this stretch you'll see multicolored layers of rock, pushed upward by tremendous forces from within the earth, followed by a side canyon, with large, arched alcoves boasting delicate curved ceilings. Head on to a view of **Timber Top Mountain,** which has a sagebrush-blanketed desert at its base, but is covered with stately fir and ponderosa pine at its peak. Watch for mule deer on the brushy hillsides, especially between October and March, when they might be spotted just after sunrise or before sunset. From here, continue to **Rockfall Overlook;** a large scar on the mountainside marks the spot where a 1,000-foot chunk of stone crashed to the earth in July 1983, the victim of erosion. And finally, stop to see the canyon walls themselves, colored orange-red by iron oxide and striped black by mineral-laden water running down the cliff faces.

Probably the least visited area of the park is between Zion Canyon and Kolob Canyons, accessible via the **Kolob Terrace Road** (also called the Kolob Road). Heading north off Utah 9 from the village of Virgin, about 15 miles west of the park's southern entrance, the Kolob Terrace Road climbs through a piñon-juniper woodlands, past grassy meadows, and finally up into a forest of tall ponderosa pines and old stands of aspen. There's a viewpoint a offering panoramic vistas across the park, a picnic area, vault toilets, and the small Lava Point Campground. Views from the road are good going up, but more dramatic coming down. This road is closed in the winter.

6 Historic & Man-Made Attractions

There are no major historic sites that you will visit at Zion National Park, but there is some archaeological evidence of the early peoples who inhabited the area, plus a few 20th-century structures of historic interest. Archeologists say that evidence has been found throughout the park of several historic and prehistoric cultures. These include people from what is called the **Archaic Period,** who are believed to have occupied the area from about 7,000 to 2,500 years ago; as well as the people of the **Virgin Anasazi Pueblo culture,** who are believed to have lived at Zion until about A.D. 1150; and finally the **Southern Paiutes,** who arrived in the area at about A.D. 1100 and stayed until European settlers arrived about 1860. Although there are no designated and marked archaeological sites, hikers with sharp eyes may see pot shards, pieces of ancient stone tools, rock art, and other artifacts. In addition, there is an excellent **rock art site** just off the east entrance approach road, and another site near the park's south entrance; ask rangers for specific directions. Park officials ask that you **refrain from touching** these artifacts—especially rock art and painted pottery, because skin oils can damage them—and that you not move them.

From the **Weeping Rock** parking area, you can see remains of a **cable operation** that was used to lower millions of board feet of timber from Cable Mountain to the floor of Zion Canyon between 1901 and 1926 (see "Cable Mountain and Deertrap Mountain Trails" in chapter 4). The timber was needed for the building of **pioneer settlements along the Virgin River.**

Along **Taylor Creek** in the Kolob Canyons section of the park are the remains of **two logging cabins.** The **Gustav Larson homestead cabin,** built in 1930 of white fir logs brought from Cedar City, is near the confluence of the North and Middle forks. A **second homestead cabin,** also built of white fir logs in 1930, but by Arthur Fife, a teacher at Southern Utah State college (now Southern Utah University), is perched on a bench above the north bank of the creek (see "Middle Fork of Taylor Creek Trail," in chapter 4).

Also from that period is the **Zion–Mt. Carmel Tunnel,** which you'll drive through if entering or leaving the park on the east side. Dedicated on July 4, 1930, the 1.1-mile tunnel cost over $500,000 and took over 3 years to build. Another historic structure, the handsome **Zion Lodge,** was built in 1925 by the Union Pacific Railroad, but was destroyed by fire in 1966. It was rebuilt the following year in its original style. Several 1920s-era **tourist cabins** are located near the lodge.

7 Ranger Programs

Park rangers present a variety of free programs and activities. **Amphitheater programs,** which sometimes include a slide show, take place most evenings at campground amphitheaters. Topics vary, but could include the animals or plants of the park; geology; the night sky, mankind's role in the park; or some unique aspect like Zion's slot canyons. Rangers also give **short talks** on similar subjects at various locations, including the Zion Lodge auditorium. Ranger-guided hikes and walks, which may require reservations, might take you to little-visited areas of the park, on a trek to see wildflowers, or out at night for a hike under a full moon. Schedules of the various activities are posted on bulletin boards at the visitor centers, campgrounds, and other locations.

For information on ranger programs geared toward children, see "Especially for Kids," below.

8　Guided Tours

Guided **horseback rides** in the park are available from Canyon Trail Rides (see chapter 4, "Hikes & Other Outdoor Pursuits in Zion National Park").

Just outside the park, guided hikes are offered by **Bike Zion,** 1458 Zion Park Blvd., Springdale (☎ **800/4SLIKROK** or 435/772-3929), starting at $35 for a 2¹/₂-hour hike, as well as multiday backpacking trips. The company also has a hiker and backpacker shuttle service.

Several **national tour operators** offer guided biking, hiking, and backpacking trips in the park area, as well as more traditional tours; see "Adventure Vacations & Organized Tours" in chapter 2, "Planning Your Trip."

9　Especially for Kids

One of the nicest things about Zion National Park is the wide variety of hiking trails, so there is usually a path suited to every family member's ability level. Among trails that children find especially enjoyable are the **Weeping Rock Trail,** because it leads to a fascinating rock that oozes water; and the various **Emerald Pools trails,** which take you to a series of attractive little pools, where you just might see—or at least hear—some frogs. The only problem at the Emerald Pools is that kids (and adults, too) have to resist the strong urge to submerge their toes in the dark green water.

Older youths—perhaps young teens—who are in good physical shape will enjoy hiking into **the Narrows** from the end of the Riverside Walk, where a hike is almost a swim, and you're staring up from the bottom of a 1,000-foot ravine. See chapter 4, "Hikes & Other Outdoor Pursuits in Zion National Park" for additional hiking information.

Park rangers also have special programs just for children. Kids up to 12 years old can join the ✪ **Junior Rangers,** participate in a variety of hands-on activities, and earn certificates, pins, and patches. Morning and afternoon sessions, each lasting 2¹/₂ hours, are daily from Memorial Day to Labor Day, with children meeting at the Nature Center in the South Campground. There's a one-time fee of $2 per child, and the age range is strictly enforced.

Kidding Around

Kids love the huge screen and dramatic photography in the *Treasure of the Gods* production at the **Zion Canyon Theatre.** See "Outdoor Pursuits & Attractions" under Springdale in chapter 8, "Gateway Towns."

Hikes & Other Outdoor Pursuits in Zion National Park

Z ion offers a wide variety of hiking trails, ranging from easy half-hour walks on paved paths to grueling overnight hikes over rocky terrain along steep drop-offs. Several free brochures on hiking trails are available at the visitor centers, and the **Zion Natural History Association** publishes several good booklets describing established trails and off-trail routes (see chapter 2). Hikers with a fear of heights should be especially careful when choosing trails—many include steep, dizzying drop-offs. Ratings here are provided by the authors and other experienced hikers, and are entirely subjective. Guided hiking and biking trips in the area are offered by several local companies, including **Zion Adventure Company,** 36 Lion Blvd., Springdale (☎ **435/ 772-3590;** www.zionadventures.com), and **Bike Zion,** 1800 Zion Park Blvd., Springdale (☎ **800/475-4576** or 435/772-3929; www.bikezion.com). National companies offering guided hiking/ biking trips in the area are discussed in chapter 2.

1 Day Hikes

Hikers have the chance to see the park from two perspectives— either a high plateau trip that looks down into the canyons, or a descent into the canyons that provides spectacular views skyward.

SHORTER HIKES

Court of the Patriarchs. 100 yards RT. Easy. Access: Court of the Patriarchs parking area along Zion Canyon Rd.

This short, steep, paved hike leads to a viewpoint that provides vistas of the Streaked Wall and the Sentinel to the south, the Court of the Patriarchs and Mount Moroni straight ahead (west), the Spearhead and Angels Landing to the north, and Mountain of the Sun and Twin Brothers above and behind (east). A footbridge crosses the river and connects to the Sand Bench Trail.

✪ **Weeping Rock Trail.** 0.5 miles RT. Easy to moderate. Access: Weeping Rock parking lot on Zion Canyon Rd.

This is among the park's shortest hikes. A self-guided nature trail, with interpretive signs explaining the natural history of the area, it takes you through a mixed forest to a rock alcove with lush hanging gardens of ferns and wildflowers. The mist that emanates from the Weeping Rock above is delightfully refreshing on a hot afternoon, and in fall the variety of colors is quite striking. Although paved, the trail is relatively steep (gaining 98 ft.) and not suitable for wheelchairs.

Canyon Overlook Trail. 1 mile RT. Moderate. Access: Parking area at the east terminus of the Zion–Mt. Carmel Tunnel.

Panoramic vistas are the lure on this self-guiding trail that takes you to an overlook offering a magnificent view of lower Zion Canyon, the East and West temples, the Towers of the Virgin, and the Streaked Wall. The trail, which is sometimes slippery because of sand, begins with a series of uneven steps cut into the sandstone. There are long drop-offs into the narrow chasm of Pine Creek Canyon, but the trail is mostly fenced. It has an elevation gain of 163 feet. Guidebooks are available at the Zion Canyon Visitor Center and at the trailhead.

✪ **Emerald Pools Trail System.** 1.2–2.5 miles RT. Easy to moderate. Access: Trailhead across from Zion Lodge.

This can be either an easy 1-hour walk or a moderately strenuous 2-hour hike, depending on how much you choose to do. A 0.6-mile paved path leads from the Emerald Pools parking area through a forest of oak, maple, fir, and cottonwood, to several waterfalls, a hanging garden, and the picturesque Lower Emerald Pool. From here, a steeper, rocky trail (not appropriate for wheelchairs) continues a quarter mile to Middle Emerald Pool; and then climbs another 0.3 miles past cactus, yucca, and juniper to Upper Emerald Pool, with another waterfall. As you climb the trail, there are views of soaring stone formations such as Lady Mountain, the Spearhead, Mount Majestic, Red Arch Mountain, Deer Trap Mountain, and the Great White Throne. From the Middle Pool there is a long drop-off leading to the Lower Pool; the Upper Pool is enclosed on three sides by sheer cliffs and on the fourth by boulders. Maple trees provide shade, and a feeling of peace pervades the area. The pools are named for the green color of the water, which is caused by algae. Total elevation gain is 69 feet to Lower Emerald Pool, 150 feet to the middle pool, and 400 feet from the trailhead to Upper Emerald Pool. Swimming or wading is not permitted in any of the pools.

Riverside Walk and the Gateway to the Narrows. 2 miles RT minimum.
Paved and easy. Access: Temple of Sinawava at the end of Zion Canyon Rd.

An easy, paved trail follows the Virgin River upstream to the beginning of the Zion Canyon Narrows, with trailside exhibits and hanging wildflowers in spring and summer. Accessible for people with disabilities with some assistance, the trail has an elevation change of only 57 feet over its 2 miles. The pavement ends at the Narrows, and here you either turn around and head back, or continue upstream into the Narrows (yes, you will get wet), where the canyon walls are sometimes less than 30 feet apart but more than 1,000 feet high. You should have a sturdy hiking staff to help keep your footing as you wade into the cold river over slippery rocks. Before entering the Narrows, check the weather forecast (posted at Zion Canyon Visitor Center) and discuss your plans with park rangers—being at the bottom of a very narrow slot canyon is definitely not a good idea in a rainstorm (common in July and August), when flash floods are a serious threat. Permits are not required for short day hikes into the

Narrows, but are required for longer treks (see "The Narrows" under "Exploring the Backcountry," below).

Hidden Canyon Trail. 2 miles RT. Moderate to strenuous. Access: Weeping Rock parking lot along Zion Canyon Rd.

A particularly scenic hike along a paved trail sometimes cut from solid stone, Hidden Canyon Trail climbs 850 feet to the mouth of a narrow water-carved canyon. You'll pass slickrock formations and sheer cliffs—stay back from the edge as they may be unstable and slippery. Walking up the dry streambed into the canyon, you'll pass grottoes and other water-formed decorations on the canyon walls, including a small natural arch about a half mile upstream from the mouth of the canyon. This trail includes long drop-offs and is not recommended for anyone with a fear of heights.

✪ **Watchman Trail.** 3 miles RT. Moderate. Access: Zion Canyon Visitor Center and Transportation Hub.

This moderately strenuous, but relatively short hike gets surprisingly little use, possibly because it can be very hot in the middle of the day. Climbing 368 feet to a plateau near the base of the Watchman formation, it offers splendid views of lower Zion Canyon, Oak Creek Canyon, the Towers of the Virgin, and the West Temple formations, plus the town of Springdale. Stay on the main trail created by the National Park Service—it's 3 feet wide—and avoid the smaller criss-cross trails created by mule deer seeking water and food. The area traversed by the trail is a spring seepage/riparian area rich with a variety of plants—walk quietly and watch for wildlife, especially birds.

West Bank of the Virgin River. 2.6 miles one-way. Easy. Access: Court of the Patriarchs Viewpoint at the south end, the Grotto Trailhead at the north end, both along Zion Canyon Rd.

A pleasant hike along the river, this trail affords continual views of Zion Canyon plus the opportunity to see a myriad of birds in the wetlands, and an occasional mule deer coming out for a drink in the early evening. After crossing the Virgin River at the Court of the Patriarchs Viewpoint, turn left into the middle of the Court and stop for a moment to gaze up at these awe-inspiring monoliths of stone. Leaving the Court, the trail turns north, levels out, and enters the riparian environment of the river, where you'll be walking amid cottonwood and box elder. As you trek northward, watch for Cathedral Mountain and Mount Majestic to slowly raise their heads above you. This section of the trail is used heavily by horseback-riding groups (see "Horseback Riding," later in this chapter), so be prepared to step aside quietly (and watch where you step).

Once past the spur leading east to Zion Lodge across Zion Canyon Road, horse traffic comes to an end, and you embark on the wide, paved trail to the Emerald Pools. Follow the main trail up, around, and down into the amphitheater holding the Lower Pool, bypassing the spur trails leading to the Upper Pools. Follow signs for the Grotto Trailhead as you leave the Lower Pool, winding through lovely rock gardens and past delightful waterfalls. As the trail angles northward again to follow the river, the Great White Throne gradually emerges into view across the river; cross the bridge to the Grotto Trailhead.

Sand Bench Trail. 3.4-mile loop. Moderate. Access: Court of the Patriarchs Viewpoint along Zion Canyon Road.

This trail is most popular with hikers in the off-season, since horseback riders use it heavily April through October. After crossing the river on the footbridge, this sandy trail turns left and meanders through a sagebrush meadow in the Court of the Patriarchs. As it's not always well-marked, watch carefully for the junction where you'll take the left fork across a small streambed, after which the 500-foot climb to the top of the bench begins. Soon the loop splits, but in terms of difficulty, there's no difference between the two. If you choose the right fork, you'll pass under sheer stone walls and stark towers, until you come out on top, where the Streaked Wall dominates the near view and the Watchman stands sentinel in the distance. As you approach the base of the Streaked Wall, you'll come to a rest area and corral that mark the end of the loop. The trail back takes you along the edge of an escarpment above the river, offering magnificent views of the Twin Brothers, Mountain of the Sun, and East Temple. Remember, horses have the right-of-way, so step to the side of the trail and stand quietly while they pass (see "Horseback Riding," later in this chapter).

Pa'rus Trail. 3.5 miles RT. Easy. Access: Either the entrance to Watchman Campground, near the amphitheater parking area; or near the Nature Center in South Campground.

This easy, paved trail (fully accessible to wheelchairs and also suitable for baby strollers) follows the Virgin River, crossing it several times, and provides views of the rock formations in lower Zion Canyon. Try to identify the West Temple, Watchman, Bridge Mountain, Sentinel, and East Temple formations. The trail has a 50-foot elevation gain and, unlike other park trails, is also open to bicycles (see "Biking & Mountain Biking," later in this chapter) and leashed pets. Watch for stop signs where the trail crosses park roads, stay alert, and be aware of vehicles whose drivers may not easily see you on the winding roads. With the closing of Zion Canyon Road to private vehicles, this trail links the campgrounds and south park entrance with the beginning of beginning of the closed section of Zion Canyon Road, and the rest of Zion Canyon.

✪ **Angels Landing Trail.** 5 miles RT. Difficult. Access: Grotto Picnic Area along Zion Canyon Rd.

A popular though strenuous hike that is most certainly not for anyone with even a mild fear of heights, this trail climbs 1,488 feet to a summit that offers spectacular views into Zion Canyon. But be prepared: The final half mile follows a narrow, knife-edge trail along a steep ridge, where footing can be slippery even under the best of circumstances.

After crossing the footbridge over the Virgin River, turn north through a riparian woodland of cottonwood, box elder, and tamarisk, above which Angels Landing beckons. The trail climbs to the mouth of Refrigerator Canyon around the west side of the monolith. Grottos and overhangs dot the red sandstone canyon walls. Shortly before reaching the head of the canyon, a series of 21 switchbacks, known as "Walter's Wiggles," have been built into a cleft in the wall. In spite of their rather whimsical name, these carefully crafted stoneworks are regarded as one of the engineering marvels of the park. At the top of the switchbacks, you begin the gradual ascent to Scout Lookout, the saddle behind Angels Landing from which you get spectacular views into Zion Canyon. This is a good turning-around point for those who want to avoid the final knife-edge hike to the top.

Here also, the West Rim Trail heads off to the left, while the Angels Landing Trail turns southeast and begins the final brutal climb along the spine of a razor-like ridge. From this point, many stretches have support chains to hold on to, but not all, and there are no guardrails on Angels Landing itself—in fact one wonders how the gnarled trees perched atop it manage to hold on. But the views are stupendous—a 360° panorama—with the Virgin River gently bending around three sides at the bottom of the canyon, the Great White Throne and Red Arch Mountain to the southeast, and the entrance to the Narrows beyond the Temple of Sinawava to the north.

Middle Fork of Taylor Creek Trail. 5.4 miles RT. Moderately strenuous. Access: Trailhead parking area along Kolob Canyons Rd., about 2 miles from Kolob Canyons Visitor Center.

You will probably get your feet wet as you hike along the rather narrow Taylor Creek and its Middle Fork, fording it several times.

Kolob Plateau Trails

Following the creek bed upstream toward the mouth of the canyon, you'll have views of Tucupit and Paria Points directly ahead and Horse Ranch Mountain to the left. The Gustav Larson cabin is near the confluence of the North and Middle forks, after which the trail begins its ascent into the canyon between Tucupit and Paria points; it levels out as it follows the creek bed. A second homestead cabin is perched on a bench above the north bank of the creek (see "Historic & Man-Made Attractions," in chapter 3). The trail ends at Double Arch Alcove, a large colorful grotto with the arch high above. The term alcove denotes an arch against rock, with no space for light to pass through. The trail has an elevation gain of 450 feet.

LONGER HIKES

✪ **East Mesa Trail.** 6 miles RT. Easy. Access: E. Mesa Trailhead. (From Zion National Park's east entrance drive 2.4 miles east on Utah 9, turn north onto the road to the North Fork and Navajo Lake—impassable when wet or snowy—and go 5.3 miles to the Ponderosa Hunting Club. Visitors should register at the small mailbox at the Ponderosa Gate—sign both in and out. Drive through the main entrance and head left [west] on Twin Knolls Rd. for about 1.2 miles to a T intersection; turn right [north] onto Beaver Rd., which deteriorates into little more than a dirt track and eventually re-enters the park at the trailhead.)

This is an easier and shorter route to Observation Point than the Observation Point Trail (see below), and is open to equestrians. The trail heads westward over a fairly open plateau through ponderosa pines and manzanita, turning a little to the south as it passes Mystery Canyon, winds around a steep unnamed canyon opening to the south into Echo Canyon, and then passes another canyon to the north that empties into the Virgin River just below the Narrows. Finally the trail connects to Observation Point Trail just 0.2 miles from its end; turn right for Observation Point. This trail ends at almost the same elevation it began, but you'll climb up 315 feet and then down again in the process.

Cable Mountain and Deertrap Mountain Trails. 6.2 miles RT to Cable Mountain, 7.8 miles RT to Deertrap Mountain, or 10.9 miles combination RT. Moderate. Access: Ponderosa Hunting Club. (From Zion National Park's east entrance drive 2.4 miles east on Utah 9, turn north onto the road to the North Fork and Navajo Lake—impassable when wet or snowy—for 5.3 miles to the Ponderosa Hunting Club. Visitors should register at the small mailbox at the Ponderosa Gate—sign both in and out. Drive through the main entrance and head left [west] on Twin Knolls Rd. for about 0.8 miles; turn left [south] onto Buck Rd. Bear right at the first Y, then left at the next Y, following signs for the Gooder-Reagan cabin. The last few hundred yards descends a rocky grade and crosses a wash, requiring a high-clearance vehicle, before entering the national park at the trailhead. Close the gate behind you to keep livestock out.)

From the Ponderosa Hunting Club Trailhead, you'll head west into an open ponderosa pine forest, which soon gives way to a meadow of sagebrush, where you join the East Rim Trail (see below), turning left for Cable and Deertrap mountains. Soon your route bears right and the East Rim Trail veers left. The trail climbs steadily through juniper, piñon, Gambel oak, and a few ponderosa pines, then leaves the trees behind before topping out in open sagebrush. Here the trail separates, the right branch for Cable Mountain and the left for Deertrap Mountain.

The **Cable Mountain Trail** climbs gently to a knoll from which you can see the more than 10,000-foot-high pink cliffs of the Virgin Rim in the distance, before descending into a manzanita and juniper forest. The trail gradually makes its way northwest along a plateau to the point where pioneers built a cable tramway to carry logs down to the Virgin River. The remains of the tram structure are fragile and very hazardous—please stay back (see "Historic & Man-Made Attractions," in chapter 3). Looking out over the Big Bend of the Virgin River you have a grand view of the Organ and Angels Landing with the ashen cliffs of Cathedral Mountain serving as a backdrop. This trail has an elevation gain of 530 feet and a loss of 460 feet.

The **Deertrap Mountain Trail** slopes downward from the junction with Cable Mountain Trail toward the head of Hidden Canyon. As you cross an open area dotted with manzanita, several paths lead to the bottom of a draw where there's a small seep. Follow the trail out onto Deertrap Mountain and to the rim of Zion Canyon for a breathtaking view of the Mountain of the Sun and the Twin Brothers practically in your lap, and the Court of the Patriarchs directly across the canyon. From here, you can walk north and south along the edge of the canyon. The better-defined path runs north (0.4 miles) to an overlook from which you can see the Great White Throne, Angels Landing, and in the distance the red tips of the Temple of Sinawava. The southern path (0.6 miles) is rough, virtually a game trail in places, and leads to a point from which you can view the East Temple and Twin Brothers. This trail has an elevation gain of 760 feet and a loss of 470 feet.

These hikes can also be done as a more relaxing overnight trip from the Ponderosa Hunting Club Trailhead; or for the really zealous, there's the option of combining these with the more strenuous East Rim Trail (see below), which adds 11.2 miles to the jaunt.

Observation Point Trail. 8 miles RT. Moderately strenuous. Access: Weeping Rock parking lot along Zion Canyon Rd.

This hike climbs over 2,000 feet to Observation Point, but if you can manage it the incredible views from this promontory make all the exertion worthwhile. As you climb the switchbacks zigzagging up the canyon wall, a variety of formations become visible from new directions. First there's Angels Landing across the Virgin River and the Organ a little closer, then the alcove containing Weeping Rock to the north, next Cathedral Mountain appears from beyond Angels Landing, and finally the sheer north face of Cable Mountain looms directly overhead. The trail levels out as it enters Echo Canyon, which alternately closes in, with steep rock walls barely an arm-span apart, and widens out, allowing more distant views of rugged peaks. When the East Rim Trail branches off to the right you head left up the north wall of Echo Canyon, climbing along steep switchbacks until the trail heads across a steep slope of white cliffs dropping 1,000 feet below the path. When you finally reach the top of the Navajo sandstone formation, the East Mesa Trail (see above) heads off to the right and you bend around to the left through deep sand to Observation Point, right at the tip of the plateau, at an altitude of 6,507 feet. From here you can see far down Zion Canyon; the Great White Throne looms in the foreground with Red Arch Mountain just beyond. For an easier hike to Observation Point, take the East Mesa Trail (see above).

East Rim Trail. 10.5 miles one-way to Weeping Rock Trailhead. Difficult. Access: Trailhead is at the end of a short paved road past a ranger's residence, 150 yards west of the east entrance to the park.

Your exertions will be rewarded with a variety of views on this challenging trail, which connects with the trails to Cable and Deertrap mountains, Observation Point, and Hidden Canyon (see trail descriptions above), before descending into Zion Canyon at the Weeping Rock Trailhead. Trail intersections are fairly well marked all along the East Rim.

The trail follows an old dirt road up the dry wash of Clear Creek and then begins a climb of about 800 feet up the narrow canyon of Cave Creek. Once on top you'll follow the rim high above Clear Creek, providing terrific views of Checkerboard Mesa. At the head of Jolley Gulch you'll find yourself at a high pour-off, looking down at water-smoothed canyon walls. Leaving the rim, the trail winds along the East Rim Plateau, through scattered piñon and Utah juniper, manzanita, and an occasional Gambel oak in wetter areas. This plateau was heavily logged in the early part of the 20th century, the wood being lowered from Cable Mountain to the Virgin River (see "Cable Mountain and Deertrap Trails," above, and "Historic & Man-Made Attractions," in chapter 3). About 5.3 miles along the trail you come to a short spur trail over to Stave Spring, a fairly dependable water source (treat before use). Soon the trail to Cable and Deertrap Mountains branches off to the left; and after another half mile the turnoff to the Ponderosa Hunting Club heads right. The East Rim Trail descends toward Echo Canyon, following the top of canyon walls for about a half mile before switch-backing down the almost sheer cliffs into Echo Canyon, and offering views of Cathedral Mountain and Angels Landing. The trail becomes a mite dicey along here, with twists and turns, ups and downs, complicated by slickrock where the only trail pointers are rock cairns. But finally you reach the junction with the steep Observation Point Trail, which takes off to the right and once on top connects to the East Mesa Trail (see above). Continuing down Echo Canyon brings you to the end of the trail at Weeping Rock Trailhead, located in Zion Canyon along Zion Canyon Road.

Chinle Trail. 16.2 miles RT. Easy to moderate. Access: From the south entrance to the park drive west on Utah 9 for 3.5 miles to a parking area on the right (north) side of the road. From here, follow a marked trail 1.4 miles through a new real estate development.

The first few miles of this quiet desert trail are fairly easy walking along a wide sandy path. Ahead you have views of Mount Kinesava and the Three Marys, and behind are the Eagle Crags. A gradual 150-foot incline brings you to the Petrified Forest, denoting the top of the Chinle Formation. (Please remember it is illegal to remove anything from the national park; leave the lovely pieces of petrified wood as you find them so that others can enjoy them also.) After crossing Huber Wash the trail heads for Scoggins Wash through more desert terrain, with the addition of juniper, piñon, and sagebrush. To the northwest you can see Cougar Mountain, and looking east allows views of the Towers of the Virgin, the West Temple, and the Sundial. Once on the mesa beyond Scoggins Wash, the trail heads for three knolls, passing through several small saddles, traversing a meadow, and crossing the Old Scoggins Stock Trail, built by the area's early pioneers. Continuing west, the trail passes between two knolls and bends around to the north, where you'll have no trouble finding an attractive campsite. The final descent into Coalpits Wash brings Cougar Mountain, Smith Mesa, and Lambs Knoll into view, and at the bottom you'll have a delightful sight of a pretty waterfall a bit upstream from Coalpits Spring—the end of the trail. This trail can be uncomfortably hot in summer, but an absolute delight from November to May, with the possibility of blankets of wildflowers to delight the eye in spring. The elevation gain of this hike is a gradual 550 feet over the first 5 miles, after which you drop about 250 feet over the last 3 miles.

Wildcat Canyon and Wildcat Canyon Connecting Trails. 8.7 miles, Hop Valley Trailhead to Lava Point Trailhead. Moderate. Access: From Virgin, head north on Kolob Terrace Rd. about 13 miles to the parking area for Hop Valley Trailhead.

A high-country trail linking the Hop Valley and West Rim trails (see section 2 below), this connector also provides access to several primitive canyon trails. The Wildcat Trail cuts east (right) just a short distance from the Hop Valley Trailhead, passing between Spendlove Knoll to the south and Firepit Knoll to the north, both extinct cinder cones. Crossing the upper end of the Lee Valley takes you through open grassy meadows sprinkled with sagebrush and Gambel oak. Vistas to the east and south include Northgate Peaks, the tops of North and South Guardian Angels above a reddish ridge, the Altar of Sacrifice, the West Temple, and Mount Kinesava. Cedar posts mark the trail as it becomes obscure in places through the valley, and after crossing the Pine Springs Wash, rock cairns point the way along an incline of slickrock.

As you reach the top of the incline you have a grand unobstructed view of North Guardian Angel. Once past the junctions with the spur to **Wildcat Canyon Trailhead** and **Northgate Peaks Trail** (the first heads left, the second right—continue straight ahead at both), you begin a gentle incline through a ponderosa pine forest continuing upward along Russell Gulch. As you enter the headwaters of Wildcat Canyon you'll see Gambel oak, bigtooth maple, and quaking aspen (see chapter 10, "A Nature Guide to Zion & Bryce Canyon National Parks"). In autumn, their wildly colorful displays contrast with the White Cliffs extending to the south and the dark strip of lava across the top of the canyon. The trail descends into the canyon, passing a dependable spring (treat the water before using), and then climbs the far wall, eventually reaching the top of the Horse Pasture Plateau. Just before the junction with the West Rim Trail, you'll have fine views of the Lava Point lookout. At the **West Rim Trail,** turn left to reach **Lava Point Trailhead,** the end of the trail. This trail has a total elevation gain of about 1,500 feet, with numerous ups and downs along the way.

2 Exploring the Backcountry

There are numerous backpacking opportunities in the park, and several of the day hikes discussed above can be more comfortably done in 2 or more days. In addition to the park's established trails and the famous Narrows, there are a number of off-trail routes for those experienced in the use of compasses and topographic maps—get information at the Zion Canyon Visitor Center & Transportation Hub. Backcountry permits ($5) are required for all overnight hikes in the park as well as slot canyon routes. Backcountry camping is not permitted within 1 mile of a road or trailhead.

Hop Valley Trail. 13.4 miles RT. Moderate to difficult. Access: Trailhead on Kolob Terrace Rd., about 13 miles north of Virgin.

This trail loses about 1,000 feet as it meanders northwest through sunny fields and past Gambel oak, partly following an old Jeep road and then a stream, before arriving at La Verkin Creek. Many hikers continue on the La Verkin Creek/Kolob Arch trails to see Kolob Arch.

The beginning of the trail takes you through some rather deep sand, so if your gear includes gaiters, wear them. After passing through the hiker gate in the fence marking the beginning of an inholding, you'll be sharing space with cattle from spring through fall. Follow the four-wheel-drive road, marked by fence posts when it becomes almost too faint to see, until you reach the stream in the bottom of the Hop Valley. Follow the stream or cattle trails along it down the valley, and shortly Langston Canyon will come in from the right, sometimes contributing a trickle of water to the stream. About a half mile farther, another fence marks the end of the inholding and the stream sinks into the sand and disappears in summer. A sign marks where the trail leaves the wash and climbs a hill, after which the trail follows a steep descent into the valley of La Verkin Creek. Camping is allowed outside the inholding, and shady sites can be found among the pines not far from the wash. From here you can head to Kolob Arch, about three-quarters of a mile away, explore the La Verkin Creek system, or return to the Hop Valley Trailhead. If you see any cattle outside the inholding, notify the Park Service when you finish your hike.

✪ **La Verkin Creek/Kolob Arch Trails.** 14 miles RT. Moderate heading east, strenuous returning west. Access: Kolob Canyons Rd. at Lee Pass.

La Verkin Creek and its tributaries are responsible for the magnificent canyons cut into the red Navajo sandstone in this section of the park. The hike passes through dry sagebrush flats and forests of conifers, cottonwoods, and box elders; and where water seeps from the stone, hanging gardens astonish the eye. The trail is popular and can be quite busy on summer weekends, in spite of the almost 800-foot net elevation gain of the return trek. From the trailhead, you descend to Timber Creek, which is often dry by late summer. Follow it upstream around the base of Shuntavi Butte, Timber Top Mountain, and Gregory Butte; as you climb into a small open bowl, the views widen to the south and east. Soon you'll come to an old corral built by Mormon pioneers, after which there is a short side hike downstream to a series of pretty, though short, waterfalls. Follow La Verkin Creek upstream along the north bank, with Gregory Butte towering overhead on your left and Neagle Ridge jutting up on the right.

When you reach the turnoff to the Kolob Arch Viewpoint, turn left along a tiny tributary with some steep ups-and-downs on rocky footing for about a half mile. Then look up—Kolob Arch soars high overhead about a quarter mile away. One of the largest arches in the world, it measures over 300 feet wide. *Caution:* Going beyond the viewpoint is not recommended due to the instability of the slopes. Back on the main trail a short way upstream, cross over to Beatty Spring, after which is the junction with **Hop Valley Trail** (heading southeast). You've come about 7 miles and descended to 5,200 feet elevation. Further exploration upstream takes you to Beartrap Canyon and then up Willis Creek, another 4.5 miles with a further elevation loss of just under 200 feet.

✪ **The Narrows.** 16 miles one-way. Difficult. Permit required (see above). Access: Chamberlain's Ranch (outside the park); arrange a shuttle for delivery and pickup. (From Zion National Park's east entrance drive 2.4 miles east on Utah 9, turn north onto the road to the North Fork and Navajo Lake—impassable when wet or snowy—and go 18 miles. Immediately after crossing the bridge over the Virgin River, turn left onto a gravel road and go 1 mile to the trailhead, which is just before the river ford.)

Hiking the Narrows is not really hiking a trail at all, but more like wading along the bottom of the North Fork of the Virgin River, through a spectacular 1,000-foot-deep chasm that, at less than 30 feet wide in spots, fulfills its name admirably. Passing fancifully sculptured sandstone arches, hanging gardens, and waterfalls, this hike is recommended for those in good physical condition who are up to fighting sometimes-strong currents. Those who want just a taste of the Narrows can walk and wade in from the other end: Follow the **Riverside Walk** (see above) from the Temple of Sinawava and continue into the water a ways.

The full trip through the Narrows involves a long-day or preferably 2-day trek, which entails arranging a shuttle to the trailhead and then transportation from the Temple of Sinawava, where you leave the canyon. From the trailhead, on private land, you'll ford the river and follow a dirt road downstream. Please remain on the road and leave all gates as found. The road ends a short distance beyond an old cabin, and from here you will hike either along or in the river, which has cut a deep canyon into the Navajo sandstone. Occasionally you might note a lone conifer leaning out from the stone wall at an absurd angle. Finally the walls are broken only by an occasional steeply ridged canyon created over millennia by some seemingly insignificant stream in its quest to reach the Virgin River. At one point you'll come up against a 12-foot waterfall, where a path circumnavigates this natural barrier by leading you through a slot in the rock.

The Narrows: Safety First

Hiking in the Narrows, which are subject to flash flooding, can be treacherous, since there are many sections where there is no place to escape a rushing wall of water. Hiking here is not advised when rain is forecast or threatening; park officials strongly recommend that hikers check the latest National Weather Service forecast before setting out, even when skies appear clear. Weather forecasts are posted at the Zion Canyon Visitor Center, and rangers are available to discuss current conditions, but park officials emphasize that all hikers are responsible for their own safety.

Even those planning just a short day hike into the Narrows, entering from the end of the Riverside Walk, need to spend some time on preparation. Hikers should wear sturdy boots or shoes with good ankle support that they won't mind getting wet; carry an empty bag to pack out all trash; take drinking water, sunscreen, and a first-aid kit; be prepared for cold temperatures with a sweater or jacket; and put everything in waterproof containers.

Experienced Narrows hikers also recommend that you take a walking stick to help steady yourself against the strong currents; sticks are usually available near the end of the Riverside Walk, and hikers should not cut tree branches. Because there are no rest rooms in the Narrows, hikers should use the rest room at the Riverside Walk Trailhead before heading out. Park officials request that human waste be buried as far away from the river and other water sources as possible.

Because of strong currents and deep pools, park officials recommend that children under 4'8" tall not hike in the river.

You are now within the boundary of the park, and in another mile and a half will reach the confluence with Deep Creek, where the canyon widens to absorb this sizable flow of water. In the next 2 miles lie the designated—and assigned—campsites. The current is faster due to the increased flow of water, and the rocks underfoot are slippery, so step carefully to avoid injury. Kolob Creek is the next tributary seen, though it flows only when waters are released from Kolob Reservoir for irrigation downstream; Goose Creek comes in next and signals a deepening of the water—waist-high in some places—and increased speed of the flow. Soon you'll see Big Springs gushing over moss-covered stone on the right wall of the canyon, signifying the beginning of the Narrows.

For the next 3 miles there is no place to climb out of the water in the event of a flash flood, and there is practically no vegetation to grab onto, as any small seedling is periodically ripped from its hold by raging waters. (See the box "The Narrows: Safety First," above.) The river spreads from wall to wall, requiring constant wading in a deep canyon with little light. The water has even undercut the walls near the confluence with Orderville Canyon. Runoff from above oozes from the canyon walls here, providing moisture for hanging gardens and habitat for the minuscule Zion snail, found nowhere else in the world (see chapter 10, "A Nature Guide to Zion & Bryce Canyon National Parks"). About a mile farther where the canyon opens out, a narrow ribbon of water slips out of Mystery Canyon above and skims down the rounded canyon wall. Just beyond, you can finally climb out of the water onto the paved **Riverside Walk** that takes you to the Temple of Sinawava and the end of the hike.

Permits ($5) are required for full-day and overnight hikes originating from Chamberlain's Ranch, which must be purchased at the Zion Canyon Visitor Center the day before your hike; campsites are assigned and the number of hikers, both day and overnight, is limited. Short day hikes, starting and ending at the end of the Riverside Walk, do not require permits.

✪ **West Rim Trail.** 28.4 miles RT. Difficult. Access: Lava Point Trailhead. (From Virgin, take Kolob Terrace Rd. north about 21 miles, turn right toward Lava Point, and after about a mile there's a fork: If it's dry, take the left fork and drive about 1.3 miles to the trailhead; otherwise, take the right fork to Lava Point Campground, where there's a connecting trail to the trailhead.)

This trail has a net elevation loss of 3,560 feet over 14.2 miles to the Grotto Picnic Area, and many hikers choose to arrange for a shuttle at one end or the other rather than attempting the strenuous climb back to Lava Point—most of the rise is achieved in the first 6 miles from the south end.

Over half of this very popular hike is spent atop the Horse Pasture Plateau, a finger of land pointing toward Angels Landing, which affords incredible vistas all along the trail. The plateau boasts a wide range of plant life and consequently a fascinating variety of birds and animals. The number of blackened hulks of trees attest to the many lightning strikes that have occurred here. Stark reminders of a terrible wildfire in 1980 can also be seen, and the results of more recent fires display man's increased knowledge of the benefits of monitored and prescribed burns.

At the southern end of the plateau, you can choose to take the **Telephone Canyon Trail** or stay on the Rim Route; the first is a little shorter and they come together again at West Rim Spring Junction, just before the steep descent into Zion Canyon. The climb down takes you around and behind Mount Majestic and Cathedral Mountain, following part of Refrigerator Canyon, and connects to **Angels Landing Trail** before depositing you at the bridge over the Virgin River near the Grotto Picnic Area.

3 Biking & Mountain Biking

Although bikes are prohibited on almost all trails, as well as forbidden to travel cross-country within the national park boundaries, Zion is among the West's most bike-friendly parks. The **Pa'rus Trail** runs a little under 2 miles along the Virgin River, from the south park entrance and South Campground to Zion Canyon Road, crossing the river and several creeks, and providing good views of the Watchman, West Temple, the Sentinel, and other lower-canyon formations. The trail is paved and open to bicyclists, pedestrians, pets on leashes, and those with strollers or wheelchairs, but is closed to cars.

Starting in the summer of 2000, the **Zion Canyon Road** beyond its intersection with the Zion–Mt. Carmel Highway will be closed to private motor vehicles, except to motorists with reservations at Zion Lodge. However, the road, formerly called Zion Scenic Drive, will be open to hikers and bicyclists, as well as shuttle buses.

Bicycles can also be ridden on other park roads, but not through the Zion–Mt. Carmel Tunnel.

Although mountain bikes are prohibited on the trails of Zion National Park (except the Pa'rus Trail), just outside the park—mostly on Bureau of Land Management and state-owned property—are numerous rugged Jeep trails that are great for mountain biking, plus more than 100 miles of slickrock cross-country trails and single-track trails. **Gooseberry Mesa,** above the community of Springdale, is generally considered the best mountain-biking destination in the area, but there are also good trails on nearby **Grafton Mesa.**

Bikers Beware

If you have a bike rack on the rear bumper of your car, make sure the bike tires are far from the exhaust pipe; an owner of one bike shop says he does a good business replacing exhaust-cooked bike tires.

Talk with the knowledgeable staff at **Bike Zion** (see intro above) about the best trails for your interests and abilities. This full-service bike shop also offers maps, a full range of bikes and accessories, repairs, and rentals ($23–$35 for a full day, $17 to $27 for a half day). The company can also arrange shuttles for you and your bike. Bike rentals are also available from **Scenic Cycles,** 180 Zion Park Blvd., Springdale (☎ 435/772-2453; www.sceniccycles.com) at similar rates.

Bike Zion offers guided mountain bike trips outside the park, starting at $35 for a 2¹/₂-hour tour; and a variety of multiday excursions, including some with catered gourmet meals or educational themes.

4 Other Summer Sports & Activities

FISHING   Though not the most popular pastime in the park, fishing in the Virgin River is permitted, with a valid Utah fishing license. Anglers occasionally catch a few trout, although the stream is not stocked.

HORSEBACK RIDING   Horseback riding is permitted in many areas of the park—it's especially popular in the Kolob Canyons section—although it is prohibited on some of the more popular hiking trails. Backcountry permits ($5) are required for overnight trips into the backcountry. For complete details, contact the visitor centers or park offices (see chapter 2, "Planning Your Trip") and ask for a copy of the free handout "Pack Animal Use."

Guided rides in the park are available March through October from **Canyon Trail Rides,** P.O. Box 128, Tropic, UT 84776 (☎ 435/679-8665; www.onpages.com/canyonrides), with ticket sales and information at Zion Lodge. A 1-hour ride along the Virgin River costs $15 and a half-day ride on the Sand Beach Trail costs $40. Riders must weigh no more than 220 pounds, and children must be at least 5 years old for the 1-hour ride and 8 years old for the half-day ride. Reservations are advised.

ROCK CLIMBING   Expert technical rock climbers like the tall sandstone cliffs in Zion Canyon, although rangers warn that much of the rock is loose, or "rotten," and climbing equipment and techniques suitable for granite are often less effective (and therefore less safe) on sandstone. Permits (free) are required for overnight climbs, and because some routes may be closed at times, such as during peregrine falcon nesting from early spring through July, climbers should check at the Zion Canyon Visitor Center before setting out. Rock climbing workshops and clinics are offered in the park area by **Zion**

Adventure Company (see intro section above), with rates starting at about $100 per person (for two or three people) for a half-day beginner's program.

Climbers without the necessary expertise for Zion are advised to try nearby Snow Canyon State Park (see chapter 9, "Nearby Things to See & Do").

SWIMMING & TUBING   Hikers in the Narrows soon find that they are participating in a water sport, as they wade along the "trail" at the bottom of the Virgin River. Tubing and wading are also permitted in other sections of the river—there is a designated river-access area just south of the South Campground amphitheater—but those going into the water should wear shoes to protect their feet. River float tubes are available for rent ($10 per day) from **Scenic Cycles** (see "Biking & Mountain Biking" above). Swimming and wading are prohibited in the Emerald Pools.

5 Winter Activities

Zion does not usually get enough snow for winter sports. Hiking is the main activity year-round, although winter hikers need to be especially careful when trails are icy.

5

Exploring Bryce Canyon National Park

*T*he scenic beauty of Bryce Canyon National Park is unsurpassed—and because it is among the West's most accessible parks, its wonders can be enjoyed by everyone from the very young to the very old, and from hearty backpackers to visitors in wheelchairs. Bryce's defining feature is its hoodoos—those rock formations that delight the child in all of us. But look a bit deeper and you'll discover Bryce Canyon's other faces, from its varied wildlife to its rugged forests.

1 Essentials

GETTING THERE/GATEWAYS   Situated in the mountains of southern Utah, the park is crossed east-west by Utah 12, with the bulk of the park, including the visitor center, accessed by Utah 63, which turns south off Utah 12 into the main portions of the park. U.S. 89 runs north-south west of the park, and Utah 12 heads east to Tropic and eventually Escalante.

VISITOR CENTER & INFORMATION   The visitor center, at the north end, just after you enter the park, has exhibits on the geology and history of the area and presents an excellent 10-minute introductory slide show on the park—a quick and painless geology lesson. There are large photos of many of the park's better-known formations, and a relief map that shows not only Bryce Canyon but also nearby sections of the Colorado Plateau, including Grand Staircase–Escalante National Monument. Rangers can answer questions and provide backcountry permits; several free brochures are available; and books, maps, videos, postcards, and posters are sold. The visitor center is open daily year-round except Thanksgiving, Christmas, and New Year's days. Summer hours are usually 8am to 8pm, with shorter hours the rest of the year.

FEES   Entry into the park (for up to 7 days) costs $10 per family or $5 for one person. A $20 annual pass is also available. In addition, from late spring through early fall, a mandatory $5 user fee for shuttle use for each family unit will be charged, plus an additional $5 user fee will be charged for those who want to take their motor vehicles into the park. These extra user fees are not covered by the Golden Eagle, Access, or Age passports. Campsites cost $10 per night.

Backcountry permits, which cost $5 and are available at the visitor center daily until 8pm, are required for all overnight trips into the backcountry, and backcountry camping is permitted on only two trails, with details at the visitor center.

REGULATIONS & WARNINGS　While most visitors to Bryce Canyon enjoy an exciting vacation without mishap, accidents can occur, and here—possibly because of the nature of the trails—the most common injuries by far are sprained, twisted, and broken ankles. Park rangers strongly recommend that hikers—even those out on short day hikes—wear sturdy hiking boots with good traction and ankle support.

Backcountry hikers should practice minimum-impact techniques; they are prohibited from building fires and must carry their own water, as water sources in the backcountry are considered unreliable. Bicycles are prohibited in the backcountry and on all trails. Feeding or molesting wildlife, vandalism, and disturbing any natural feature of the park are all prohibited. Pets, which must be leashed at all times, are prohibited on all trails, in the backcountry, and in public buildings.

Trailers are not permitted beyond Sunset Campground; they can be left in a campsite, at the visitor center, or in other designated parking areas. Any vehicle longer than 25 feet (large trucks and motor homes, for instance) cannot go to Paria View.

A concern in the park in recent years has been **bubonic plague,** which, contrary to popular belief, is treatable with antibiotics if caught early. The bacteria that causes bubonic plague has been found on fleas in prairie dog colonies in the park, so you should avoid contact with wild animals, especially prairie dogs and other rodents. Those taking pets into the park should dust them with flea powder. Avoiding contact with infected animals will greatly minimize the chances of contracting the plague, but caution is still necessary.

Symptoms, which generally occur from 2 to 6 days after exposure, may include high fever, headache, vomiting, diarrhea, and swollen glands. Anyone with these symptoms following a park visit should get medical attention immediately, because the plague can be fatal if not treated promptly.

Bryce Canyon National Park

FAST FACTS

ATMs Just outside the entrance to the park, there is an automated teller machine (ATM) in the lobby of Ruby's Inn (☎ 435/834-5341).

Car Trouble/Towing Services Located just outside the entrance to the park, **Bryce Canyon American Car Care Center** (☎ 435/834-5232) is a full-service station, with facilities to work on large vehicles and motor homes, and offers AAA towing service (☎ 435/834-5222), a car wash, and car rentals.

Emergencies Dial ☎ **911,** call the Garfield County Sheriff's office (☎ 435/676-2411), or contact a park ranger.

Gas Stations Just outside the entrance to the park are two gas stations (Chevron and Texaco) operated by Ruby's Inn; the Chevron gas pumps are open around the clock for those who pay by credit card. There are also gas stations along Utah 12 in Bryce and Tropic.

Laundry Inside the park there is a coin-operated laundry at the General Store, about a quarter mile south of North Campground near the Sunrise Point parking area. It's open daily from mid-April to October.

Just outside the entrance to the park, Ruby's Inn has two coin-operated laundries. The one in the main complex is open 24 hours a day year-round, and the second, located at Ruby's Campground about a quarter mile south of the inn, is open from April to October from 7am to 9:30pm daily.

Medical Services There is a first-aid station at Bryce Canyon Lodge. The closest hospital is the **Garfield Memorial Hospital and Clinic,** 224 N. 400 E. in Panguitch, 24 miles northwest via Utah 12 and U.S. 89 (☎ **435/676-8811**), which has a 24-hour emergency room.

Permits Permits are required for backcountry camping. They cost $5 and are available at the visitor center until 8pm daily.

Post Offices Inside the main building of Ruby's Inn is the Bryce Post Office (ZIP 84764). The Bryce Canyon Lodge also has a post office (Bryce Canyon, ZIP 84717), open from April through October.

Supplies   There is a small general store (contact **Bryce Lodge** ☎ 435/834-5361) inside the national park that is open from mid-April to October, with groceries and camping supplies, plus snacks, film, ice, beer, bundles of firewood, and souvenirs, and all at surprisingly reasonable prices. Hours are 8am to 8pm daily, although these are flexible and the store is sometimes open a bit longer in summer, with shorter hours at the beginning and end of the season.

On the south side of the lobby of **Ruby's Inn** (☎ 435/834-5341), just outside the entrance to the park, is a huge general store that offers souvenirs, western clothing, camping supplies, and a good selection of groceries. The store is open 7:30am to 10:30pm daily. In the lobby is a small liquor store, a car-rental desk, a beauty salon, a 1-hour film processor, and tour desks where you can arrange excursions of all sorts, from horseback and all-terrain–vehicle rides to helicopter tours.

There's also a grocery store and bakery at **Foster's,** 1$^{1}/_{2}$ miles west of the park entrance road on Utah 12; and a grocery store, with a deli and camping supplies. The lowest prices in the area are at the grocery store at **Doug's Place Country Inn Motel,** 120 N. Main St., in Tropic, about 8 miles east of the park entrance road along Utah 12 (☎ 435/679-8633).

Telephones   Public telephones are located at the visitor center, Bryce Canyon Lodge, Sunset Campground pay station, and the General Store. There is also a public phone at Ruby's Inn, just north of the park entrance.

Weather Updates   For current statewide weather information, contact the **National Weather Service** (☎ 801/524-5133; http://nimbo.wrh.noaa.gov/saltlake). For local weather information, call the park office (☎ 435/834-5322).

2 Tips from a Park Ranger

Dave Mecham, who has worked at the park for more than a dozen years in a variety of capacities, says it's easy to pinpoint Bryce Canyon's most striking feature—it's the hoodoos.

"They're photogenic, stunningly beautiful. You can find free-standing rock formations throughout the world, but I don't think there's any place where hoodoos are this numerous, this delicately eroded, or beautifully colored."

But what Mecham enjoys most about the park is not necessarily its most recognizable feature. He prefers standing on the rim and

Wildlife Viewing

Bryce Canyon has a wide variety of wildlife, ranging from mule deer—which seem to be almost everywhere—to the often seen golden-mantled ground squirrel and Uinta chipmunk. Also in the park are black-tailed jackrabbits, coyotes, striped skunks, and deer mice. Occasionally visitors catch a glimpse of a mountain lion, most likely on the prowl in search of a mule-deer dinner. Elk and pronghorn may also be seen at higher elevations.

The Utah prairie dog, listed as a threatened species, is actually a rodent and not a distant canine relative. It inhabits park meadows in busy colonies and can be fascinating to watch. However, don't get too close because its fleas may carry disease (see "Regulations & Warnings," earlier in this chapter).

Of the many birds in the park, you're bound to hear the obnoxious call of the Steller's jay. Other birds often seen include violet-green swallows, common ravens, Clark's nutcrackers, American robins, red-shafted flickers, dark-eyed juncos, and chipping sparrows. Watch for white-throated swifts as they perform their exotic acrobatics along cliff faces. The park is also home, at least part of the year, to peregrine falcons, red-tailed hawks, golden eagles, bald eagles, and great horned owls.

The Great Basin rattlesnake, although pretty, should be given a wide berth. Sometimes growing to more than 5 feet long, this rattler is the park's only poisonous reptile. Happily, like most rattlesnakes, it is just as anxious as you are to avoid a confrontation. Other reptiles you may see are the mountain short-horned lizard, tree lizard, side-blotched lizard, and northern sagebrush lizard.

For detailed information on many of these animals, plus the various plants you'll encounter in the park, see chapter 10, "A Nature Guide to Zion & Bryce Canyon National Parks."

simply relishing the views: "Looking out from the rim of Bryce, across the hoodoos, it seems you can see forever. The atmospheric conditions are almost ideal, and you get the feeling that you're looking at a piece of America that's still pretty wild, and just hasn't changed much through time."

✪ **Bryce Amphitheater** has the best scenery in the park, in Mecham's opinion: "It's the place in the park where everything's coming together geologically to carve hoodoos at their best." Mecham particularly enjoys the **Rim Trail** that runs along the edge of the canyon and highly recommends the section between Inspiration and Bryce Points, with perhaps the very best view from a section known as **Upper Inspiration Point,** which is 300 to 400 yards south of Inspiration Point.

Among Mecham's favorite trails is the ✪ **Fairyland Loop,** which takes about 4 hours: "I think it's a fantastic trail." To get the best views, start at Sunrise Point, go down past Tower Bridge, and back up through Fairyland Canyon to Fairyland Trailhead. Then take the Rim Trail back to Sunrise Point. "It's 5 miles below the rim and then 3 miles of Rim Trail. Fairyland Canyon is beautiful—the highlight of that loop—and as you come around the bend, you're hiking straight toward a really beautiful backdrop. If you're going the opposite direction, you have to keep stopping to look over your shoulder."

Mecham calls Bryce Canyon a "morning park," because, with only a few exceptions, the views are much better illuminated by early morning light than at any other time of day. To get the most out of your visit, he recommends spending at least 1 night at or near the park: "If you're spending the night close by, I think it would be a big mistake to miss sunrise—in the middle of the summer that's getting up before 6."

Getting up early is also the best way to avoid crowds, according to Mecham, since most people don't get to the viewpoints or onto the trails until about 10am. The other way to avoid crowds is to walk away from them. Mecham says that you're likely not to see anyone at all on the park's two backcountry trails at the south end of the park; but avoiding crowds, even in the park's most popular areas, often takes only a short walk. "**Sunset Point** is probably the busiest place in the park, especially in midsummer at midday," he says. "You finally get a parking spot, then walk out to a very crowded viewpoint, where you're standing shoulder to shoulder—it's real hectic—but if you take a 5-minute walk south along the Rim Trail toward Inspiration Point, you'll leave the people immediately—they just cluster at those views."

Mecham says that September and October are probably the best times to visit the park. "It's still busy," he says, "but less crowded on

A Tip for Picnickers

On a hot summer day, the best spot in the park for a picnic lunch is Rainbow Point, where you'll find picnic tables and rest rooms. It's also among the coolest areas because, at 9,115 feet elevation, it's the highest point in the park.

trails." However, if you really want to avoid people, you'll feel you have the park all to yourself if you visit midweek in the middle of the winter. "We plow the roads so people can drive to the viewpoints and photograph the canyon with snow on it, and the people that ski or snowshoe will enjoy it the most." He adds, "Skiing is at its best in January and February, when it's really cold."

3 The Highlights

Everyone should spend at least a little time on the park's **scenic drive,** as it follows the canyon rim south to Rainbow Point. There are numerous stops where you can get off the shuttle or out of your vehicle and gaze into the canyon to view the varicolored formations and trailheads that provide access down into the amphitheaters. (For more information on this and other drives, see "Seeing the Park by Car," below; also check out chapter 6, "Hikes & Other Outdoor Pursuits in Bryce Canyon National Park," where you'll find detailed information on all the hiking trails and activities mentioned in this section).

Another top experience is walking the **Rim Trail** for at least a short way, to access different views into Bryce Amphitheater. Although it's worthwhile at any time of day, the Rim Trail is especially wonderful just after sunrise, in time to catch the changing angles of the sun on the hoodoos.

One viewpoint not to be missed is the appropriately named ✪ **Inspiration Point,** which provides a splendid view down into Bryce Amphitheater, the park's largest and most colorful natural amphitheater. It provides the best view of **Silent City,** which is packed with hoodoos and leads the imagination to unexpected heights. Some of us, however, believe the view is even better— possibly the best in the park—just south of Inspiration Point along the Rim Trail, up a little rise, at what is usually called **Upper Inspiration Point.**

To really get a feel for the canyon and grand close-up views of many spectacular formations, you must hike down into it to walk among the hoodoos. Among the various trails from which to choose, one of the best is the **Queen's Garden Trail,** which can be completed in only a few hours, is easy enough for most park visitors— including children—and takes you to some fascinating hoodoos.

Speaking of hoodoos, there are a few that are on almost everyone's must-see list. These naturally sculpted monuments in stone include majestic **Queen Victoria,** which can be seen from Sunrise Point on the rim but is better examined from the Queen's Garden Trail.

Rest Rooms at Bryce Canyon

The nicest and most modern rest rooms at Bryce Canyon are at the visitor center and just off the lobby at Bryce Lodge. They're well maintained, heated, and have flush toilets and sinks with hot water.

There are also rest rooms with hot water at the General Store in the park, and just outside the park entrance at Ruby's Inn (just off the lobby).

Other park facilities range from flush toilets at North and Sunset Campgrounds and Sunset Point, to vault toilets at Rainbow, Yovimpa, and Farview points. Although there are few toilets along trails (none in the backcountry), you will find a vault toilet on the Peekaboo Loop Trail, just west of its intersection with the Bryce Point cutoff trail.

Although essentially outhouses, vault toilets—officially called "bulk-reduction toilet systems"—have come a long way in the past 20 years—they're now clean, sanitary, and best of all they don't smell. However, there is no water for hand washing, no lights, and no heat. During busy times, the less-developed rest room facilities may run out of toilet paper, so it's best to carry a backup source.

Another is magnificent **Thor's Hammer,** which is visible from Sunset Point but best seen from the Navajo Loop Trail. For a discussion of the geologic forces that form hoodoos, see chapter 10, "A Nature Guide to Zion & Bryce Canyon National Parks."

Attractions that aren't made of stone include Bryce Canyon's **bristlecone pine trees,** exceptionally old evergreens that grow in some of the more inhospitable areas of the park. They're easily seen via the Bristlecone Loop Trail. See chapter 10, "A Nature Guide to Zion & Bryce Canyon National Parks."

4 How to See the Park in 1 or 2 Days

It would be easy to spend a week in Bryce Canyon, starting with the visitor center, then moving along the scenic drive, a few short walks, and then advancing to more serious hikes. But what makes this park so attractive to many of us is that there are ways to see a good deal of Bryce in a short amount of time.

Get an early start, stopping first at the **visitor center,** of course, where you can watch the short slide show that explains some of the area's geology—the *why* and *how* of Bryce. Then either drive the

18-mile (each way) dead-end **park road,** stopping at viewpoints to gaze down into the canyon (see "Seeing the Park by Car," below), or hop on the **Bryce Canyon Scenic Tours & Shuttles** van for a 2-hour guided tour, complete with lively commentary (see "Guided Tours," below).

An alternative is to take the new **shuttle system,** which will take you to most of the main viewpoints. Whichever way you choose to get around, spend at least a little time at **Inspiration Point,** which offers a splendid (and yes, inspirational) view into **Bryce Amphitheater** and its hundreds of statuesque pink, red, orange, and brown hoodoo stone sculptures.

After seeing the canyon from the top down, it's time to get some exercise; so walk at least part way down the **Queen's Garden Trail.** If you can spare 3 hours, hike down the **Navajo Loop Trail** and return to the rim via **Queen's Garden Trail** (both are described in the next chapter). Those not willing or physically able to hike into the canyon can enjoy a leisurely walk along the **Rim Trail,** which provides spectacular views down into the canyon. That evening, try to take in the campground amphitheater program.

5 Seeing the Park by Car

The park's **18-mile scenic drive** (one-way) follows the rim of Bryce Canyon, offering easy access to a variety of views into the fanciful fairyland of stone sculptures below. Trailers are not permitted on the road but can be left at several parking lots. Also, because all overlooks are on your left as you begin your drive, it's best to avoid crossing traffic by driving all the way to the end of the road and stopping at the overlooks on your return. Allow 1 to 2 hours for the main viewpoints; 3 to 4 hours if you plan to do a bit of walking.

After leaving the visitor center, drive 18 miles to **Yovimpa** and **Rainbow Point** overlooks, which offer expansive views of southern Utah, Arizona, and sometimes even New Mexico. From these pink cliffs, you can look down on a colorful platoon of stone soldiers, standing at eternal attention. The short **Bristlecone Loop Trail** (described in the next chapter), from Rainbow Point, leads to an **1,800-year-old bristlecone pine,** believed to be among the oldest living things at Bryce Canyon. Heading north, the **Black Birch Canyon Overlook** is a roadside pullout where you get a good view of the southern part of the park, including Rainbow Point.

From here, drive back north to **Ponderosa Canyon Overlook,** where you can gaze down from a dense forest of spruce and fir at multicolored hoodoos, before continuing to **Agua Canyon Overlook,** with some of the best color contrasts you'll find in the park. Looking almost straight down, watch for a hoodoo known as **the Hunter,** with a hat of green trees.

Now continue on to **Natural Bridge,** actually an arch carved by rain and wind, that spans 85 feet. From here, continue to **Farview Point,** where there's a panoramic view to the distant horizon and the Kaibab Plateau at the Grand Canyon's north rim. From Farview Point, a dirt path leads several hundred yards north to **Piracy Point,** which offers good views to the north. After passing the **Swamp Canyon** overlook, continue until you see a right turn off the main road, where you'll find three viewpoints.

The first of these is **Paria View,** with views to the south of the White Cliffs, which have been carved into light-colored sandstone by the Paria River.

Driving Tip

The scenic drive is practically deserted in early mornings—any time before 9am—which is also the best time to see deer, and when the light on the hoodoos is the richest.

To the north of Paria View, you'll find **Bryce Point,** a splendid stop for seeing the awesome **Bryce Amphitheater,** the largest natural amphitheater in the park, as well as distant views of the Black Mountains to the northeast and Navajo Mountain to the south.

From here it's just a short drive back toward the main road and **Inspiration Point,** a must-see offering views similar to those at Bryce Point plus the best view in the park of the **Silent City,** a sleeping city cast in stone.

Now return to the main road and head north to **Sunset Point,** where you can see practically all of Bryce Amphitheater, including the aptly named **Thor's Hammer** and the 200-foot-tall cliffs of **Wall Street.**

Continue north to a turnoff for your final stop at **Sunrise Point,** where there's an inspiring view into Bryce Amphitheater. This is the beginning of the **Queen's Garden Trail,** an excellent choice for even a quick walk below the canyon's rim (described in the next chapter).

6 Historic & Man-Made Attractions

Although prehistoric Indians and 19th-century pioneers spent some time in what is now Bryce Canyon National Park, they left little evidence. The park's main historic site is the handsome sandstone and ponderosa pine ✪ **Bryce Canyon Lodge,** built by the Union Pacific Railroad and opened in 1924. Much of it has been faithfully restored to its 1920s appearance, and the lobby contains historic photos taken in the park during that period.

7 Ranger Programs

Park rangers present a variety of free programs and activities. **Evening programs,** which may include a slide show, take place most evenings at campground amphitheaters. Topics vary, but could include such subjects as the animals and plants of the park, geology, and mankind's role in the park's early days. Rangers also give half-hour talks on similar subjects several times daily at various locations in the park, and lead hikes and walks, including a **moonlight hike** (reservations required) and a wheelchair-accessible, 1-hour **canyon**

Wildlife Alert

For a good chance to see peregrine falcons, go to Paria View, sit quietly away from the crowds, and then look out over the amphitheater, where peregrine falcons can often be spotted.

rim walk. Schedules are posted on bulletin boards at the visitor center, general store, campgrounds, and Bryce Canyon Lodge.

Several times a week from spring through fall, usually in the evening, a talk is given on the patio or in the auditorium at **Bryce Canyon Lodge.** The free talks often include some lodge history, geology of the area, and discussion of some of the park's trails. Check at the lodge or visitor center for the current schedule.

8 Guided Tours

Bryce Canyon Scenic Tours & Shuttles (☎ **800/432-5383;** www.brycetours.com) offers 1¹/₂- to 2-hour tours year-round; these leave from Ruby's Inn just outside the park entrance. A general tour, stopping at several viewpoints, costs $24 for adults, $12 for children aged 5 to 15, and free for those under 5. The sunrise/sunset tours cost $26. Combination and other specialized tours can be arranged.

For a bird's-eye view of the canyon and its numerous formations, contact **Bryce Canyon Helicopter Scenic Flights** (ask for the flight desk at Ruby's Inn, ☎ **435/834-5341**). Tours last from less than 20 minutes to more than an hour, and the longer trips include surrounding attractions. Prices range from $55 to $225, and passengers weighing less than 100 pounds are charged half.

Several national **adventure tour operators** offer guided biking, hiking, and backpacking trips in and near the park, and other companies offer more traditional tour packages. See "Adventure Vacations & Organized Tours" in chapter 2, "Planning Your Trip."

9 Especially for Kids

Bryce Canyon is a fantasyland that kids love—even teenagers trying their hardest to be bored will have a great deal of trouble not being fascinated by the bizarre and whimsical shapes that in many ways are the essence of this park. Among the best trails for kids are **Queen's Garden** and **Navajo Loop,** which are not only fairly easy, but lead to some of the park's best hoodoos. Teenagers with a bit more stamina will probably enjoy the 8-mile **Fairyland Loop.** Details are available in the "Day Hikes" section of chapter 6.

During the summer, children 12 and younger can join the **Junior Rangers,** participate in a variety of programs, and earn certificates and patches ($1). Junior Ranger booklets are available at the visitor center. In addition, park rangers periodically conduct **special kids' activities**—usually lasting about an hour and a half—on subjects such as the park ecology. Reservations are required, with information at the visitor center.

6

Hikes & Other Outdoor Pursuits in Bryce Canyon National Park

*O*ne of the wonderful things about Bryce Canyon is that even though hiking is the best way to explore, you don't have to be an advanced backpacker to really get to know the park. Many people also see the park on mule or on horseback, and on a few bike rides along the scenic drive en route to the trailheads. In the winter, the park's trails are opened up to snowshoers and cross-country skiers.

Several national adventure tour operators offer guided hiking and backpacking trips in and near the park; see "Adventure Vacations & Organized Tours" in chapter 2, "Planning Your Trip."

1 Day Hikes

Remember that all trails below the rim have at least some steep grades, so you should wear hiking boots with a traction tread and good ankle support to avoid ankle injuries, the most common accidents in the park. During the hot summer months, you'll want to hike either early or late in the day. Not only is it cooler then, but there are fewer people on the trails and the lighting on the hoodoos can produce dramatic effects. Bryce's rangers have recently stopped rating hiking trails as to their difficulty, saying that what is easy for one person may be difficult for another. Ratings here are provided by the authors and other experienced hikers, and are entirely subjective.

SHORTER HIKES

✪ **Bristlecone Loop Trail.** 1 mile RT. Easy. Access: The trailhead is located at the Rainbow Point parking area at the end of the scenic drive.

An easy walk entirely above the canyon rim, this trail winds among white fir, Douglas fir, and ponderosa and bristlecone pines. You'll see more of the latter here than on any other park trail. More than many other species, the bristlecone can withstand the strong winds and harsh conditions often found on high ridges, as well as times of prolonged drought; consequently, they often live to a great age—one in California is more than 4,000 years old! The oldest bristlecone pines in Bryce Canyon have been around nearly 2,000 years. The trail has an elevation change of 100 feet, and the round-trip takes about 1 hour.

Hat Shop Trail. 4.6 miles RT. Difficult. Access: The trailhead is located at the Bryce Point Overlook.

This is a strenuous hike with a 900-foot elevation change; it's also the beginning of the **Under the Rim Trail** (see "Exploring the Backcountry," below). Leaving the rim, you'll drop quickly to the Hat Shop, so-named because it consists of a series of formations that resemble hard, gray hats perched on narrow, reddish-brown pedestals. The trail offers close-up views of gnarled ponderosa pine and Douglas fir, as well as distant panoramas across the Aquarius Plateau toward the Grand Staircase–Escalante National Monument (see chapter 9, "Nearby Things to See & Do"). This hike will take you approximately 4 hours if you go the whole distance.

Mossy Cave Trail. 0.8 miles RT. Easy. Access: The trailhead is located along Utah 12, about 3$\frac{1}{2}$ miles east of the park access road, Utah 63.

An often-overlooked trail located outside the main part of the park, the Mossy Cave Trail offers an easy and picturesque walk. The trail follows an old irrigation ditch up a short hill to a shallow cave, where seeping water nurtures the cave's namesake moss. Just off the trail, you'll also see a small waterfall. Elevation gain is 150 feet. Allow about 45 minutes for the whole trip.

✪ **Navajo Loop Trail.** 1.4 miles RT. Moderate. Access: The trailhead is signposted at the central overlook at Sunset Point.

This trail descends from the canyon rim 521 feet to the bottom of the canyon floor and back up again. Traversing graveled switchbacks, it affords terrific views of several impressive formations, including the towering skyscrapers of Wall Street, the awesome Twin Bridges, and the precariously balanced Thor's Hammer. The round-trip on this trail takes 1 to 2 hours.

A great choice for getting down into the canyon and seeing the most with the least amount of sweat is to combine Navajo Loop with the **Queen's Garden Trail** (see below). The total distance is just under 3 miles, and most hikers take from 2 to 3 hours. It's best to start at the Navajo Loop trailhead at Sunset Point and leave the canyon on the less steep Queen's Garden Trail, returning to the rim at Sunrise Point, a half mile north of the Navajo Loop Trailhead.

The map legend shows:
- △ Campground
- ⛱ Picnic area
- 🚻 Restrooms
- ● Viewpoint
- ■ Point of Interest
- ⋯⋯ Hiking Trail
- - - Horse/Hiking Trail

✪ **Queen's Garden Trail.** 1.8 miles RT. Moderate. Access: The trailhead is located on the south side of Sunrise Point.

This short trail, which drops 320 feet below the rim, takes you down into Bryce Amphitheater, with rest benches near the formation called **Queen Victoria.** At the beginning of the descent, keep an eye cocked to the distant views so you won't miss Boat Mesa, the Sinking Ship, the Aquarius Plateau, and Bristlecone Point. As you plunge deeper into the canyon, the trail passes some of the park's most fanciful formations, including majestic Queen Victoria herself, for whom the trail and this grouping of hoodoos were named, plus the Queen's Castle and Gulliver's Castle. The round-trip takes 1 to 2 hours.

Combining the Queen's Garden Trail with the **Navajo Loop Trail** (see above) is an excellent and relatively easy way to see many magnificent hoodoos in what many believe is one of the park's most scenic areas.

Hoodoo Photography: The Light Stuff

The delightful rock formations that decorate the amphitheaters at Bryce Canyon National Park beg to be photographed, and they have been—many times and from every conceivable angle. Look at those expensive, glossy calendars or the various coffee table books filled with dramatic photos of the American West. You'll see Bryce Canyon's hoodoos standing tall in almost every single one of them, with their vibrant reds and oranges accented by the rich greens of junipers and piñons, set against a pure blue sky.

This scenery is why you came, and among the best souvenirs you can take home are good quality photos that you've taken yourself. Surprisingly, it isn't all that difficult to get calendar-quality images. A top-quality 35mm or larger format camera helps, of course; but you can get amazingly good photos even with an inexpensive point-and-shoot camera, if you simply take your photos when the light is best and take the time to carefully compose the image you want your camera to record.

Professional photographers are always carrying on about getting the right light, and at Bryce Canyon this is especially important. That's because of the nature of the hoodoos. In early morning (and to a somewhat lesser degree in late afternoon), the low angle of the sun brings out the richness of the rocks' colors—especially the reds and oranges—and emphasizes shadows, creating a multidimensional scene. On the other hand, around noon, with light coming straight down, the hoodoos look washed out and flat.

LONGER HIKES

✪ **Fairyland Loop Trail.** 8 miles RT. Difficult. Access: The trailhead is located at the Fairyland Point Overlook, off the park access road north of the visitor center; the trail is also accessible from Sunrise Point.

From Fairyland Point, this strenuous but little-traveled trail descends into Fairyland Canyon, then meanders up, down, and around Boat Mesa, crosses Campbell Canyon, passes Tower Bridge junction—a short, 200-yard side trail takes you to the base of Tower Bridge—and begins a steady climb to the Chinese Wall. About halfway along the wall, the trail begins the serious ascent back to the top of the canyon, which it reaches near Sunrise Point. To complete the loop, follow the Rim Trail back through juniper, manzanita, and Douglas fir to Fairyland Point, a trip that will take you approximately 5 hours. The loop has an elevation change of about 900 feet.

Choosing a location isn't difficult. There are plenty of spots along the Rim Trail for early morning shots; those looking for sunset photos should head down the Rim Trail past Inspiration Point, where it climbs a small hill, for the best angles. Those with telephoto or zoom lenses have the advantage of being able to get a variety of shots from one location along the rim; for close-ups and unique angles, you'll want to hike below the rim, and a wide-angle lens will often produce the best results. Some photographers like to use polarizing filters to bring out the colors of the rocks and deepen the blue of the sky.

A tripod is useful, especially when the light is a bit dim, to minimize vibration and help keep the camera from moving while you find the right composition. Those without tripods can steady their cameras by folding or balling up a jacket or sweater, resting it on a railing or other solid object, and holding the camera against it.

While at Bryce Canyon, you're apt to see photographers loaded down with expensive equipment, with all manner of lenses and filters; and although these tools can be helpful (and fun), the most important element of photography is not the equipment, but the photographer. The way to get good photos of Bryce Canyon's hoodoos with practically any type of camera is simple: Choose your timing for the best lighting—usually sunrise—compose carefully, and keep your camera steady.

Peekaboo Loop Trail. 6.8 miles RT. Difficult. Access: The trailhead is located at the Bryce Point Overlook parking area.

This trail, open to both those on foot and on horseback, winds among hoodoos below Bryce and Inspiration points. It's a fairly strenuous hike, with an elevation change of 800 feet. You follow the Under the Rim Trail briefly toward the Hat Shop, but soon you'll turn left and head toward the Peekaboo Loop. This section of the trail is narrow and often littered with rocks, so place your feet carefully. Fairly steep inclines and descents alternate with more level stretches; stop frequently to take in both the close and distant vistas. At times you can see far to the east beyond Bryce Canyon toward the Aquarius Plateau, Canaan Mountain, and the Kaiparowits Plateau; alternately, enjoy the closer prospect of the unusual Wall of Windows, the Three Wisemen, the Organ, and the Cathedral.

Hiking Tip

The lower you drop below the rim, the hotter it gets; so carry water and dress in layers that can be easily removed and carried as the temperature rises.

Various connecting trails make Peekaboo easily accessible. There's a corral and vault toilets toward the Bryce Point end of the loop. The trail is used by the park's horseback ride concessionaire from spring through fall, and hikers should step aside to let horseback riders through. Hiking the entire trail takes 3 to 4 hours.

✪ **Rim Trail.** 11 miles RT. Easy to moderate. Access: The N. Trailhead is at Fairyland Point, the S. Trailhead is at Bryce Point; the trail is also accessible from Sunrise, Sunset, and Inspiration points, and numerous other locations in between.

The Rim Trail, which does not drop into the canyon but offers splendid views from above, meanders along the rim with a total elevation change of 550 feet. This is more of a walk than a hike, and includes a half-mile section between two overlooks—Sunrise and Sunset—that is suitable for wheelchairs. Overlooking Bryce Amphitheater, the trail offers excellent views almost everywhere and is a good choice for an early morning or evening walk, when you can watch the changing light on the rosy rocks below. Another advantage is that you can access the trail from many locations, so you can have a short or long walk. You may also find this a convenient trail if you just want to simply rush out to the rim for a quick look at sunrise over the hoodoos. For some, the absolutely best view in the park is from the Rim Trail, south of Inspiration Point. If you do the whole thing, it's a maximum of 5 to 6 hours.

Sheep Creek Trail. 6–10 miles RT (3 miles takes you to the park boundary and another 2 miles brings you to the national forest boundary). Easy to moderate. Access: The trailhead sign and parking area are 5 miles south of the visitor center on the scenic drive.

This trail takes you down into the canyon bottoms, and if you continue, right out of the park into the Dixie National Forest. The first mile is on the rim, then the trail descends along Sheep Creek draw, below pink limestone cliffs toward the canyon bottom, traversing part of the Under the Rim Trail along its way. Watch signs carefully; the route can be confusing. The trail has up to a 1,250-foot elevation change, and it will take you about 5 hours if you go just to the park boundary, 8 hours if you go to the end.

2 Exploring the Backcountry

For diehard hikers who don't mind rough terrain, Bryce has two backcountry trails, usually open in the summer only. The really ambitious can combine the two for a week-long excursion. Permits, which cost $5 and are available at the visitor center, are required for all overnight trips into the backcountry.

✪ Riggs Spring Loop Trail. 8.8 miles RT. Moderate to difficult. Access: The trailhead is located on the south side of the parking area for Rainbow Point.

This hike can be completed in 4 or 5 rigorous hours, or it can be more comfortably done as a relaxing overnight backpacking trip. This relatively little-used trail offers a good opportunity to escape humanity, plus the possibility of seeing wildlife, possibly even a glimpse of an elusive mountain lion (see chapter 10, "A Nature Guide to Zion & Bryce Canyon National Parks"). The trail goes through a deep forest of Douglas fir and ponderosa pine early on, and then turns south through a burned-out area, past blackened trees and brush to the brink of the Pink Cliffs, where you can gaze into a valley of hoodoos below. Yovimpa Pass Campground, about 2 miles into the hike, occupies a tree-rimmed meadow with views of Molly's Nipple and No Man's Mesa. The descent from Yovimpa Pass follows the bed of Podunk Creek, crossing the wash several times, and traversing a forest of ponderosa and piñon pines, aspen, Douglas fir, and manzanita, before turning toward Riggs Spring and the Riggs Spring Campground (3.4 miles from the trailhead). The spring is on the west side of the trail and encircled by a wood rail fence. The trail next turns north, following Mutton Hollow and crossing several washes, finally arriving at Corral Hollow Campground at the base of the Promontory, just beyond a small stand of maple trees. (You've come 5.7 miles at this point.) The trail now begins the loop around the Promontory, sometimes crossing draws that provide clear views of the white and pink cliffs soaring above. Once around the southern tip of the promontory, the trail begins the steady return ascent to the rim of the canyon. The elevation change of the hike is 1,675 feet.

Under the Rim Trail. 22.6 miles one-way. Moderately strenuous. Access: The trailhead is located on the east side of the parking area for Bryce Point Overlook.

Running just below the rim between Bryce and Rainbow points, the Under the Rim Trail has numerous, fairly steep inclines and descents, with an overall elevation change of 1,500 feet. There are five camping areas along the route, plus a group camp area. Doing this whole trail should take you 2 to 3 days.

Although the trail doesn't move too far from the scenic drive, its location below the rim gives hikers a feeling of being alone in the wilderness. There are several spurs connecting this trail to the scenic drive, which enables hikers to choose a route to match their abilities and time schedule. The **Sheep Creek Trail** (9.5 miles from the trailhead) and **Swamp Canyon Connecting Trail** (10.4 miles from the trailhead) both lead to the Swamp Canyon Overlook and parking area on the scenic drive. **Whiteman Connecting Trail** (12.3 miles from the trailhead) takes hikers to a picnic area on the scenic drive; and **Agua Canyon Connecting Trail** (16.9 miles from the trailhead) connects to Ponderosa Canyon Overlook and parking area on the scenic drive. However, once you determine your route, it is written on your overnight pass; and you cannot change your campsite, so plan carefully.

From Bryce Point, the trail meanders toward Merrell Hollow across almost empty meadows with an occasional twisted conifer and a few manzanita. Nearing the hollow you'll see least chipmunks darting about gathering food, and you'll have grand vistas of the Aquarius Plateau, with Tropic Valley nestled in the foreground. The pinnacles grouped at the head of the hollow are brilliantly painted in purples, reds, and oranges. As you descend a long slope, you'll see the Hat Shop ahead (see "Hat Shop Trail," above); continuing the descent you'll finally arrive at Right Fork Camping Area (3 miles from the trailhead) located in a tall stand of ponderosa pines.

From Right Fork, the trail follows a deep wash through low brush to Yellow Creek, which it follows upstream, passing the Yellow Creek Group Camp (4 miles from the trailhead). As you continue upstream in this arid climate, you'll pass desert shrubs and barrel cactus among the junipers (see chapter 10, "A Nature Guide to Zion & Bryce Canyon National Parks"), and in the occasional spaces between the trees you can see the colorful spires at the top of the valley. Near the stream source is the Yellow Creek Camping Area (5.4 miles from the trailhead) in a grove of tall pines; shortly after you leave the campground the trail climbs a slope with grand views to the east, where gray cliffs provide a backdrop for deep red formations of sandstone.

The trail next passes through open pine forests, along washes, and up and down valleys, offering varying views of carved and etched walls, square-topped pillars, and a mountain topped with sharp pinnacles. Rock cairns mark the trail when it begins to fade. Once across the Sheep Creek Trail and wash, you'll wind around, up, and then down into the Swamp Canyon bottoms, where cool air pools and aspens grow. After the Right Fork Swamp Canyon Camp (10.5 miles from the trailhead), you'll climb onto the top of the plateau, pass an amphitheater filled with lovely hoodoos, and arrive at Swamp Canyon Camp (12.2 miles from the trailhead), high above the canyon floor.

As you continue, the trail heads in a southerly direction, descending into the upper basin of Willis Creek, climbing into a sandy saddle, and then descending into Bridge Canyon—look to the west for a clear view of Natural Bridge. Once in the canyon bottom the trail arrives at Bridge Canyon Camp (15.6 miles from the trailhead), nestled among pine trees. Although cliffs are visible from the campground, the Natural Bridge is blocked from view.

After crossing an open meadow that's blanketed with a profusion of yellow wildflowers in late summer, you'll follow Agua Canyon upstream—rock cairns help keep you on course. As you approach the head of the wash, you'll start up a steep, north-facing incline partially shaded with Douglas fir. As you near the crest, the trees thin out, providing magnificent views north and west.

Dropping into the next basin, you pass under a colorful cliff, after which the trail climbs several ridges and skirts a bowl filled with hoodoos, before arriving at the small Iron Spring Camping Area ($19^1/_2$ miles from the trailhead). Next you'll climb a gradual but constant slope toward the rim, with increasingly panoramic views of the orange cliffs north to Bryce Point. Soon a turn to the west blocks this vista, and you have a steep climb to achieve the rim and the Rainbow Point parking area, the end of the trail, where you'll find a picnic area and rest rooms. Rainbow Point is also the trailhead for the Bristlecone Loop and Riggs Spring Loop trails (see above).

3 Other Summer Sports & Activities

BIKING   Bikes are prohibited on all trails, as well as forbidden from traveling cross-country within the national park boundaries. This leaves the park's established scenic drive, which is open to road or mountain bikers, although you need to be aware that the 18-mile road through the park is narrow and winding, and can be crowded with motor vehicles during the summer.

Because mountain bikers are not welcome on national park hiking trails, you'll have to leave Bryce in search of trails. Fortunately, you won't have to go far—the **Dixie National Forest,** which abuts the park, has numerous mountain biking opportunities (see chapter 9, "Nearby Things to See & Do").

Mountain bikes can be rented across the street from **Ruby's Inn** (☎ **435/834-5341**) for $5 an hour, $15 for up to 4 hours, or $25 for a full day. Repairs are also available.

FISHING   The closest fishing hole to the park is at **Tropic Reservoir** in the Dixie National Forest (see chapter 9, "Nearby Things to See & Do").

HORSEBACK RIDING   To see Bryce Canyon the way early pioneers did, you need to look down from a horse or mule. **Canyon Trail Rides,** P.O. Box 128, Tropic, UT 84776 (☎ **435/679-8665;** fax 435/679-8709; www.onpages.com/canyonrides), offers a close-up view of Bryce's spectacular rock formations from the relative comfort of a saddle, and welcomes first-time riders. They have a desk inside Bryce Lodge. A 2-hour ride to the canyon floor and back costs $26.50, including tax, per person, and a half-day trip farther into the canyon costs $40 per person. Rides are offered, weather permitting, from April through November.

Although the entire park is open to cross-country skiers, rangers warn that it's extremely dangerous to try to ski on the steep—and often slick—trails leading down into the canyon.

Guided rides are also provided by **Ruby's Scenic Rim and Outlaw Trail Rides** (☎ **800/679-5859** or 435/834-5280), at Ruby's Inn, at similar rates; in addition, Ruby's offers a full-day ride with lunch for $75. There are age and weight limits, and reservations are recommended for both companies. Ruby's will also board your horse, starting at $8 per day.

4 Winter Activities

Bryce is beautiful in the winter when the white snow creates a perfect frosting on the red, pink, orange, and brown statues standing proudly against the cold winds.

CROSS-COUNTRY SKIING   Cross-country skiers will find several marked, ungroomed trails (all above the rim), including the **Fairyland Loop Trail,** which leads 1 mile through a pine and juniper forest to the Fairyland Point Overlook. From here you can take the 1-mile **Forest Trail** back to the road, or continue north along the rim for another 1.2 miles to the park boundary.

There are also connections to ski trails in the adjacent national forest (see "Dixie National Forest" in chapter 9, "Nearby Things to See & Do").

Stop at the visitor center for additional trail information, and go to **Best Western Ruby's Inn,** just north of the park entrance (☎ **435/834-5341;** see "Tropic & Bryce—Where to Stay" in chapter 8, "Gateway Towns"), for information on cross-country ski trails and snowmobiling opportunities outside the park. Ruby's grooms over 30 miles (50 kilometers) of ski trails, and also rents cross-country ski equipment.

SNOWSHOEING   Those who brought snowshoes may use them anywhere in the park except on cross-country ski tracks.

7

Where to Stay & Eat in the Parks

*A*lthough you don't have as many choices for lodging, dining, and camping inside these parks as you do at larger national parks, such as Yellowstone and Grand Canyon, to our thinking, what is offered at Zion and Bryce Canyon is a perfect compliment to your national park experience. In addition to being well managed, the Zion and Bryce Canyon lodges, as well as the National Park Service campgrounds, offer incredible views and a rustic, rugged, mountain atmosphere that can't be beat.

1 Where to Stay in Zion National Park

Room tax is about 9% in the park. Pets are not accepted at the lodge, but are allowed in the campgrounds.

✪ **Zion Lodge.** Zion National Park, UT. ☎ **435/772-3213.** Fax 435/772-2001. Information and reservations: AmFac Parks & Resorts, 14001 E. Iliff Ave., Suite 600, Aurora, CO 80014. ☎ 303/297-2757. Fax 303/338-2045. www.amfac.com. 121 units. A/C TEL. $85–$95 double; $116–$126 suites; $95–$105 cabins. AE, DISC, MC, V.

This handsome lodge was built in 1925 by the Union Pacific Railroad, destroyed by fire in 1966, and rebuilt the following year in its original style. The only lodging within the park boundaries, Zion Lodge offers a perfect location and several choices for type of accommodation. Situated in a forest with spectacular views of the park's rock cliffs, the charming cabins each have a private porch, stone (gas-burning) fireplace, two double beds, pine walls, and log beams. The comfortable motel units are basic, with two queen-size beds and all the usual amenities except televisions. Each has a private balcony. Modern motel suites, very plush and spacious, have one king-size bed, a separate sitting room with a queen-size hide-a-bed, and a refrigerator.

Ranger programs are offered in the lodge auditorium. A gift shop sells everything from postcards and T-shirts to top quality silver-and-turquoise American Indian jewelry. There is no swimming pool. The lodge fills quickly during the summer, so make reservations as far in advance as possible.

2 Camping in Zion National Park

The two developed **national park campgrounds** in Zion Canyon are the best places to camp while visiting the park, if you can find a site. A reservation system for Watchman Campground was begun in 1998 (☎ 800/365-2267). Reservations can be made up to 20 days prior to arrival, and a reservation charge of $2.50 per site per night will be added to the regular camping fee. Some campers without reservations stay at nearby commercial campgrounds their first night in the area, then hurry into the park the next morning, circling like vultures until a site becomes available.

Both of Zion's main campgrounds—**South** and ✪ **Watchman**—are located just inside the park's south entrance. They have paved roads, well-spaced sites, lots of trees, and that national park atmosphere you came here to enjoy. There are rest rooms with flush toilets, and sites for those with disabilities. Although there are no RV hookups at South Campground, electric hookups are available in two loops in Watchman. **Lava Point,** a free primitive campground with six sites, is located on the Kolob Terrace. It has fire grates, tables, and vault toilets, but no water.

There are no showers in the national park, but the commercial campgrounds listed below offer showers, for a fee, to those camping in the park.

3 Camping Near Zion National Park

Just outside the east and south park entrances are commercial campgrounds with hot showers and RV hookups. Keep in mind that the park's visitor center, campgrounds, and most of its developed attractions are closer to the south entrance than the east.

Mukuntuweep RV Park & Campground, located about a quarter mile east of the east entrance to Zion National Park on Utah 9 (P.O. Box 193, Orderville, UT 84758; ☎ 435/648-2154; www.expressweb.com/zionpark), has some shade trees, grassy tent sites, a fishing pond, a playground, and a game room, plus great views of the surrounding rocks. See "East Entrance Gateway to Zion National Park" in chapter 8, "Gateway Towns."

Zion Canyon Campground is on Zion Park Boulevard a half mile south of the park's south entrance (P.O. Box 99, Springdale, UT 84767; ☎ 435/772-3237; fax 435/772-3844). Although quite

Amenities for Each Campground, Zion National Park

Campground	Elev.	Total Sites	RV Hookups	Dump Station	Toilets	Drinking Water	Showers	Fire Pits/ Grills	Laundry	Public Phone	Reserve	Fees	Open
Lava Point	7,900	6	0	no	yes	no	no	yes	no	no	no	Free	May–Oct
South	4,000	126	0	yes	yes	yes	no	yes	no	yes	no	$10	Apr–Sept
Watchman	4,000	231	50+	yes	yes	yes	no	yes	no	yes	yes	$10–$14	Year-round
Mukuntuweep	6,000	150	30	yes	yes	yes	yes	yes	yes	yes	yes	$14–$19	Year-round
Zion Canyon	3,800	202	102	yes	yes	yes	yes	yes	yes	yes	yes	$15–$20	Year-round

crowded in summer, the campground is clean and well maintained, with tree-shaded sites and grassy tent areas. It has shade trees, some sites along the Virgin River, cable TV hookups, and a store.

In addition to the two commercial campgrounds discussed here, there is also camping at Cedar Breaks National Monument and Snow Canyon State Park (see chapter 9, "Nearby Things to See & Do").

4 Where to Eat in Zion National Park

Those looking for picnic supplies won't find any stores inside Zion National Park, but Springdale, just outside the park's south entrance, has several. There's also a small store just outside the east entrance to the park. See Fast Facts entry for "Supplies" in chapter 3, "Exploring Zion National Park."

Zion Lodge. Zion National Park. ☎ **435/772-3213.** Dinner reservations required in summer. Breakfast $2.95–$5.95; lunch $4.95–$9.95; main dinner courses $8.95–$19.95. AE, DC, DISC, MC, V. Daily 6:30–10am, 11:30am–3pm, and 5:30–9pm. AMERICAN.

Large windows facing the park's magnificent rock formations complete the dining room's mountain lodge atmosphere. Among the house specialties are an excellent slow-roasted prime rib au jus, and the very popular Utah red mountain trout. The menu also includes St. Louis–style pork back ribs, broiled salmon, and several chicken dishes, such as a skinless chicken breast basted with a spicy Caribbean sauce and served with a red onion relish. There are also vegetarian items on the menu, such as pasta marissa and black bean ragout. Ask about the lodge's specialty ice creams and other exotic desserts. At lunch you'll find the trout, barbecued pork ribs, several dinner salads such as chicken Caesar salad and Grecian vegetarian salad, and burgers and sandwiches. The usual American selections are offered for breakfast, plus omelets, fruits, and bagels. The restaurant offers a children's menu and full liquor service, and will pack lunches to go.

Zion Lodge Snack Bar. Zion National Park. ☎ **435/772-3213.** $2–$8. No credit cards. Daily 7am–9pm. AMERICAN FAST FOOD.

Located at the north end of the lodge, this simple fast food restaurant offers hot dogs, burgers, sandwiches, ice cream, frozen yogurt, and similar fare.

5　Where to Stay in Bryce Canyon National Park

Room taxes add about 9% to the total cost. Pets are not accepted at the lodge, but are allowed in park campgrounds.

✪ **Bryce Canyon Lodge.** Bryce Canyon National Park, UT. ☎ **435/ 834-5361.** Information and reservations: AmFac Parks & Resorts, 14001 E. Iliff Ave., Suite 600, Aurora, CO 80014. ☎ 303/297-2757. Fax 303/338-2045. www.amfac.com. 114 units in motel rms. and cabins; 3 suites and 1 studio in lodge. TEL. $85–$95 motel double; $95–$105 cabin; $119–$129 lodge unit. AE, DISC, MC, V. Closed Nov–Mar.

This sandstone and ponderosa pine lodge, which opened in 1924, is the perfect place to stay while exploring Bryce Canyon National Park. Its location, near the Rim Trail, is ideal for watching the play of changing light on the rock formations at various times of the day.

Guests can choose from three types of accommodations. The luxurious lodge suites are wonderful, with white wicker furniture, ceiling fans, and separate sitting rooms. The motel units, on the other hand, are simply pleasant, modern motel rooms, with two queen-size beds and either a balcony or patio. The best choice is one of the cabins. They're not large, but have two double beds, high ceilings, stone (gas-burning) fireplaces, and log beams—you might call the ambiance "rustic luxury." The lobby contains desks for horseback riding and other activities, and a gift shop offers everything from postcards and souvenirs to a fine selection of Indian pawn jewelry. There is no swimming pool. Try to reserve 4 to 6 months in advance.

6　Camping in Bryce Canyon National Park

The two campgrounds at Bryce are typical of the West's national parks. Campers get easy access to trails, plenty of trees for that genuine "forest camping" experience, but limited facilities. ✪ **North Campground** has 105 sites and **Sunset Campground** has 111 sites. Sunset Campground is open May to September only, but a section of North Campground is open year-round. North Campground is also closer to the Rim Trail, making it easier to rush over to catch those amazing sunrise and sunset colors. Get to the park early to claim a site (usually by 2pm in the summer).

Showers ($2) and a coin-operated laundry, open 7am to 8pm, are located at the **General Store** (for information, contact Bryce Canyon Lodge ☎ 435/834-5361), although it's a healthy walk from either campground. The park service operates an RV dump station ($2 fee) in the summer.

Amenities for Each Campground, Bryce Canyon National Park

CAMPGROUND	ELEV.	TOTAL SITES	RV HOOKUPS	DUMP STATION	TOILETS	DRINKING WATER	SHOWERS	FIRE PITS/ GRILLS	LAUNDRY	PUBLIC PHONE	RESERVE	FEES	OPEN
North	7,700	105	no	no	yes	yes	no	yes	no	no	no	$10	Year-round
Sunset	8,000	111	no	no	yes	yes	no	yes	no	no	no	$10	May–Sept
Bryce Canyon Pines	7,600	39	24	yes	yes	yes	yes	yes	yes	yes	yes	$16–$21	Apr–Oct
Bryce Canyon Resort	7,600	48	28	no	yes	yes	yes	no	yes	yes	yes	$5–$16	Apr–Oct
Bryce Pioneer Village	7,600	15	15	yes	yes	yes	yes	yes	no	yes	yes	$10–$15	Mid-Apr to Oct
King's Creek (USFS)	8,000	34	no	yes	yes	yes	no	yes	no	yes	no	$8	Mem. Day to Labor Day
Red Canyon (USFS)	7,400	36	no	yes	yes	yes	yes	yes	no	no	no	$9	Apr–Oct
Ruby's Inn RV Park	7,600	227	127	yes	yes	yes	yes	yes	yes	yes	yes	$14–$23	Apr–Oct
Kodachrome	5,800	24	no	yes	yes	yes	no	yes	no	yes	yes	$13	Year-round

7   Camping Near Bryce Canyon National Park

Just north of the entrance to the park is ✪ **Ruby's Inn RV Park & Campground,** Utah 63 (P.O. Box 22), Bryce, UT 84764 (☎ **435/834-5301** or 435/834-5341; fax 435/834-5481; www. rubysinn.com), along the park's new shuttle bus route. Campsites here are mostly shady and attractive. The campground contains a game room, horseshoes, a swimming pool, and a store with groceries and RV supplies. A lake and a horse pasture are nearby.

Bryce Canyon Resorts, at the junction of Utah Highways 12 and 63 (P.O. Box 640006, Bryce, UT 84764; ☎ **800/834-0043** or 435/834-5351; fax 435/834-5256), offers low-cost tent and RV campsites with RV hookups. There are no trees or grass, but it's a great location—at the staging area for the new Bryce Canyon shuttle. There's also a motel and restaurant on the property.

Bryce Pioneer Village, 80 S. Main St. (Utah 12) (P.O. Box 119), Tropic, UT 84776 (☎ **800/222-0381** or 435/679-8546; fax 435/679-8607; www.bpvillage.com), is a small motel/cabins/campground combination in nearby Tropic, with some shade trees and easy access to several restaurants. Dump-station use costs $3. Showers are available to noncampers for $2.

Bryce Canyon Pines, milepost 10, Utah 12 (P.O. Box 640005, Bryce, UT 84764; ☎ **800/892-7923** or 435/834-5441; fax 435/834-5330; bcpines@colorcountry.net), is part of a motel/restaurant/store/campground complex about $3^{1}/_{2}$ miles west of the park entrance road. The campsites, set back from the highway behind a gas station and store, are interspersed among ponderosa pines and junipers, with wildflowers and grasses. Campers have access to the motel swimming pool across the street. Those not camping here can get showers for $2.50.

King's Creek Campground, in the Dixie National Forest (mailing address 82 N. 100 E., Cedar City, UT 84720; ☎ **435/865-3700**) above Tropic Reservoir, has graded gravel roads and sites nestled among tall ponderosa pines. The nearby reservoir has two boat ramps (see "Dixie National Forest" in chapter 9, "Nearby Things to See & Do"). To get to the campground from the park, head west on Utah 12 about $2^{1}/_{2}$ miles to the access road, turn south (left) and follow signs to Tropic Reservoir for about 7 miles to the campground.

About $9^{1}/_{2}$ miles west of the park is another Dixie National Forest campground, **Red Canyon Campground** (contact the Dixie

National Forest, 82 N. 100 E., Cedar City, UT 84720; ☎ **435/865-3700** or direct to the campground 435/676-8608). Nestled among the trees along the south side of Utah 12, it offers terrific views of the red rock formations across the highway, although there is a bit of road noise. Showers cost $2.

Kodachrome Basin State Park (see chapter 9, "Nearby Things to See & Do"), about 22 miles southeast of the park, has an attractive campground with sites scattered among unusual rock "chimneys" and piñon and juniper trees.

8   Where to Eat in Bryce Canyon National Park

Picnickers can stock up at the small General Store inside the park or at one of the several stores not far from the park entrance. See the Fast Facts entry for "Supplies" in chapter 5, "Exploring Bryce Canyon National Park."

✪ **Bryce Canyon Lodge.** Bryce Canyon National Park. ☎ **435/834-5361.** Reservations required for dinner. Breakfast $3.75–$6.25; lunch $4.95–$8.95; dinner $11.50–$19.95. AE, DC, DISC, MC, V. Daily 6:30am–4:30pm and 5:30–9:30pm. Closed Nov–Mar. AMERICAN.

The dining room is delightful: the quintessential mountain lodge, with two large stone fireplaces, American Indian weavings and baskets, a huge 45-star 1897 American flag, and large windows looking out at the scenery. But the food's good, too—and reasonably priced considering that this is the only real restaurant actually in the park. House specialties at dinner include an excellent slow-roasted prime rib au jus and broiled chicken breast. Also recommended is the fresh mountain trout. There are several vegetarian items on the menu, such as lasagna and black bean stuffed pepper. Ask about the lodge's specialty ice creams and desserts, such as the exotic (and very tasty) wild "Bryceberry" crumb cake and the excellent caramel apple cheesecake. At lunch you'll find the trout, plus burgers, sandwiches, stew, and salads. All the usual American selections are offered for breakfast. Service is attentive and friendly, but a bit too speedy at dinner. The restaurant will pack lunches to go, and offers a children's menu and full liquor service.

8

Gateway Towns

*A*s development is kept to a minimum inside the national parks (except for the highly recommended Zion and Bryce Canyon lodges), you'll probably be heading to the nearby gateway communities for at least some of your dining, lodging, and entertainment needs. Outside Zion, Springdale boasts a summer theater and multimedia amphitheaters; and just beyond the boundary to Bryce are its Old Town shops and petting zoo. In addition, these gateway communities offer outdoor recreation opportunities plus provide wide choices for both lodging and dining, in price as well as style.

1 Springdale & Virgin

Settled in 1862, the small community of Springdale, population about 350 and at an elevation of 3,800 feet, is the south gateway and major lodging center for visitors to Zion National Park.

The community of Virgin (population 375) lies about 13 miles west of Springdale along Utah 9. First named Pocketville because of the closeness of the surrounding red sandstone cliffs, the town was renamed for the Virgin River that runs through it. The Kolob Terrace Road heads north out of Virgin into Zion National Park, accessing several backcountry trails.

ESSENTIALS   In an **emergency,** dial ☎ **911.** For additional information about the area contact the **Zion Canyon Chamber of Commerce,** P.O. Box 331, Springdale, UT 84767-0331 (☎ **888/ 518-7070** or 435/772-3757; www.zionpark.com); or **Utah's Southwest Color Country,** P.O. Box 1550, St. George, UT 84771-1550 (☎ **800/233-8824** or 435/628-4171; fax 435/673-3540; www.colorcountry.org).

OUTDOOR PURSUITS & ATTRACTIONS

Hiking and mountain biking are popular activities around Springdale. Visit **Bike Zion,** 1800 Zion Park Blvd., Springdale (☎ **800/475-4576** or 435/772-3929; www.bikezion.com) for advice, bike rentals, and guided tours (see chapter 4, "Hikes & Other Outdoor Pursuits in Zion National Park").

Apart from outdoor recreation, virtual nature and live music and theater attract national park visitors.

The Grand Circle: A National Park Odyssey, a multimedia production presented on a 24-by-40-foot screen in the outdoor Obert C. Tanner Amphitheater, is an excellent introduction to the national parks and monuments of southern Utah and northern Arizona. Using a state-of-the-art sound and projection system, and with the cliffs of Zion National Park in the background, the 1-hour program gives a brief look at the geology of the area, but devotes most of its time, sounds, and sights to the awe-inspiring scenery. Showings are scheduled at dusk 3 or 4 nights each week from late May to early September. Tickets cost $4 for adults, $3 for students and children under 12, and $10 per family.

The amphitheater, located just off Zion Park Boulevard, is also the venue for a variety of **concerts** and other live productions each summer, ranging from the annual Utah Symphony pops concert in late June or early July, to bluegrass, country, and acoustic performances, plus a fun-filled melodrama. Tickets cost about $8. For information, contact **Dixie College** in St. George (☎ **435/652-7994**).

You'll find an even bigger screen—some six stories high by 80 feet wide—at **Zion Canyon Theatre,** just outside the south entrance to Zion National Park at 145 Zion Park Blvd. (☎ **435/772-2400**). Here you can see the dramatic film "Zion Canyon—Treasure of the Gods" with thrilling scenes of the Zion National Park area, including a hair-raising flash flood through Zion Canyon's Narrows and some dizzying bird's-eye views. Admission costs $7 for adults and $4.50 for children 3 to 11. Shows begin hourly, 364 days a year: April through October from 9am to 9pm, and November through March from 11am to 7pm. The theater complex also contains a tourist information center, ATM, picnic area, gift and souvenir shops, food emporium, and bookstore.

For live theater, head to downtown Springdale and **The Bumbleberry Playhouse** at the Bumbleberry Restaurant & Gift Shop, 897 Zion Park Blvd. (☎ **435/772-3611**), which presents a variety of old fashioned melodramas and comedies, each summer from Memorial Day to early October. Performances are scheduled several evenings each week, with admission costing $6.50 for adults and $5.50 for children under 12 and seniors 65 and older.

WHERE TO STAY

Room tax is about 10%; pets are not accepted unless otherwise noted.

Best Western Zion Park Inn. 1215 Zion Park Blvd., Springdale, UT 84767.
☎ **800/934-7275** or 435/772-3200. Fax 435/772-2449. 120 units. A/C TV
TEL. Apr–Oct $88–$94 double, $110–$160 suites and family units; Nov–Mar
$58–$68 double, $85–$125 suites and family units. AE, DC, DISC, MC, V. Pets
accepted for a fee at management discretion.

Rooms in this handsome two-story complex are tastefully appointed
in Southwest style, with two double beds, two queens, or one king-
size bed. The grounds are beautifully landscaped, with phenomenal
views of the area's red rock formations. Facilities include a heated
outdoor swimming pool and hot tub, restaurant serving three meals
daily, gift shop, convenience store, guest laundry, liquor store, and
conference and meeting rooms.

Bumbleberry Inn. 97 Bumbleberry Lane, Springdale, UT 84767. ☎ **800/
828-1534** or 435/772-3224. Fax 435/772-3947. www.bumbleberry.com.
E-mail: bumbleberry@southernutah.com. 47 units. A/C TV TEL. Apr–Oct
$62–$77 double; Nov–Mar $49–$62 double. DISC, MC, V.

Set back from the main highway, the Bumbleberry offers large, quiet
rooms at a good price. Furnishings are simple but more than ad-
equate, with a desk in addition to a table and two chairs, and prints
depicting the area's scenery. Most rooms contain two queen-size
beds and tub/shower combinations, although five rooms have one
queen bed and shower only. Facilities include indoor racquetball, an
arcade, indoor Jacuzzi, heated outdoor pool, and an adjacent restaurant that serves three meals daily (see "Where to Dine," below).

Canyon Ranch Motel. 668 Zion Park Blvd. (P.O. Box 175), Springdale, UT
84767. ☎ **435/772-3357.** Fax 435/772-3057. 21 units. A/C TV. Apr–Oct
$58–$78 double; Nov–Mar $44–$54 double. AE, DISC, MC, V. Pets accepted
at management discretion.

Consisting of a series of two- and four-unit cottages set back from
the highway, this motel has the look of 1930s-style cabins on the
outside while providing modern motel rooms inside. Rooms are either new or newly remodeled, and options include one queen- or
king-size bed, two queens, or one queen and one double. Some
rooms have showers only, while others have shower/tub combos.
Kitchen units are also available. Room 13, with two queen-size beds,
offers spectacular views of the Zion National Park rock formations
through its large picture windows; views from most other rooms are
almost as good. The units surround a delightful lawn with trees and
picnic tables; an outdoor swimming pool and whirlpool are also
available.

Canyon Vista Bed & Breakfast at Zion. 2175 Zion Park Blvd. (P.O. Box
351), Springdale, UT 84767. ☎ **435/772-3801.** www.canyonvista.net.

Gateways to Zion & Bryce Canyon

2 units. A/C TV TEL. $100 double (tax included). Rates include continental breakfast. DISC, MC, V. Pets accepted.

Unusual among bed-and-breakfast inns, Canyon Vista not only allows guests to bring their children and pets, but also encourages them! Offering what innkeepers Leslie and Roger Coleman call a "home away from home," the inn's two spacious studio suites are decorated with country oak furnishings and local artwork, with a modern, Southwest look. Each suite has a king-size bed, queen-size hide-a-bed, and a comfortable living area with a TV/VCR combo (with movie videos) and a stereo. There's a fully equipped kitchenette (complete with coffee, tea, and popcorn), a working desk with a phone with data port, and the bathroom has a shower/tub combo, robes, and a good selection of toiletries.

The grounds combine Xeriscape landscaping with a formal garden, a deck, a large outdoor hot tub, and a pasture that abuts the Virgin River. There are spectacular views in almost every direction. Breakfast, delivered to the room, includes fresh-baked sweet breads, orange juice, granola, fruit, yogurt, hot and cold cereals, and hot beverages. A snack is served each afternoon, including biscuits for pets. Turndown service is provided. There's a telescope for night viewing of stars, and a computer with Internet access, plus fax and photocopy services are available.

Cliffrose Lodge & Gardens. 281 Zion Park Blvd. (P.O. Box 510), Springdale, UT 84767. ☎ **800/243-UTAH** or 435/772-3234. Fax 435/772-3900. www.cliffroselodge.com. 36 units. A/C TV TEL. Summer $88–$145 double. Lower rates in the winter. AE, DISC, MC, V.

With river frontage and 5 acres of lawns, shade trees, and flower gardens, the Cliffrose offers a beautiful setting just outside the entrance to Zion National Park. The modern, well-kept rooms have all the standard motel appointments, with unusually large bathrooms with shower/tub combinations. On the lawns, you'll find comfortable seating, including a lawn swing, plus a playground and a large outdoor heated pool. Guests have use of a self-service laundry.

Desert Pearl Inn. 707 Zion Park Blvd., Springdale, UT 84767. ☎ **888/828-0898** or 435/772-8888. Fax 435/772-8889. www.desertpearl.com. E-mail: info@desertpearl.com. 61 units. A/C TV TEL. $70–$150 double. AE, DISC, MC, V.

This imposing property offers luxurious and comfortable accommodations with beautiful views of the area's scenery from private terraces or balconies. Spacious rooms are decorated in modern Southwest, with either two queens or one king bed. Units also have a data port on the phone, refrigerators, microwaves, wet bars, and bidets. The grounds are nicely landscaped, and facilities include a huge outdoor heated pool and hot tub. Plans call for construction of a restaurant, gift shop, and additional units.

Driftwood Lodge. 1515 Zion Park Blvd., Springdale, UT 84767. ☎ **888/801-8811** or 435/772-3262. Fax 435/772-3702. www.driftwoodlodge.net. 47 units. A/C TV TEL. Apr–Oct $72–$82 double; $102–$110 family unit. Nov–Mar $62–$72 double; $92–$100 family unit. All rates include continental breakfast. AE, DC, DISC, MC, V. Pets accepted at management's discretion.

Beautiful lawns and gardens enhance this attractive, well-kept motel—a quiet, lush complex perfect for sitting back and admiring the spectacular rock formations that practically surround the town. Extensively renovated in 1994, the spacious rooms have white walls and light wood-grain furnishings; many have patios or balconies. Your room will have one queen, one king, or two king beds, and the two family suites each have one king-size and two queen beds. There's an outdoor heated pool with a sundeck, a whirlpool tub, and an art gallery and gift shop, but no restaurant on the premises. There is, however, a convenience store with a soup and salad bar, snacks, and drinks.

El Rio Lodge in Zion Canyon. 995 Zion Park Blvd. (P.O. Box 204), Springdale, UT 84767. ☎ **888/772-3205** or 435/772-3205. Fax 435/772-2455. www.elriolodge.qpg.com. E-mail: elrio@infowest.com. 11 units. A/C TV. Summer $47–$52 double; $60 suite. Lower rates in winter. AE, DISC, MC, V. Pets accepted for a $10 fee.

Built in the early 1960s, the El Rio is a mom-and-pop operation with one suite, five rooms upstairs, and five downstairs, all offering private bathrooms and tub/shower combos. Although small, the rooms are clean and comfortable, with light-colored walls and simple but attractive decor. There are two double beds in the upstairs rooms, with an outdoor walkway and porch affording terrific views of Zion Canyon. The downstairs rooms each have one queen bed. The suite has its own private parking area, refrigerator, extra-large bathroom, and use of the yard, with great views of the rock walls of Zion Canyon. Although there are no phones in the rooms, a public phone is available outside.

✪ **Flanigan's Inn.** 428 Zion Park Blvd. (P.O. Box 100), Springdale, UT 84767. ☎ **800/765-7787** or 435/772-3244. Fax 435/772-3396. 39 units. A/C TV TEL. Mid-Mar to Nov $79–$99 double; Dec to mid-Mar $49–$69 double. Rates include continental breakfast. AE, DISC, MC, V.

A mountain-lodge atmosphere pervades this very attractive complex of natural wood and rock, set among trees, lawns, and flowers just outside the entrance to Zion National Park. Parts of the inn date to 1947, but all rooms were completely renovated in the early 1990s, with Southwest decor, wood furnishings, and local art. One room has a fireplace; other units have whirlpool tubs and bidets; and kitchenettes are available. You might actually want to spend some time here, unlike some other options in the area, which are simply good places to sleep at the end of long days spent exploring Zion. Flanigan's has a heated outdoor swimming pool, spa, and its own nature trail leading to a hilltop vista. An on-site restaurant serves dinner (see "Where to Dine," below). Summer reservations are often booked 3 to 4 months in advance.

Harvest House Bed & Breakfast at Zion. 29 Canyon View Dr. (P.O. Box 125), Springdale, UT 84767. ☎ **435/772-3880.** Fax 435/772-3327. www.harvesthouse.net. 4 units. A/C. $80–$100 double. Rates include full breakfast. DISC, MC, V. Children over 6 are welcome.

This Utah territorial-style house was built in 1989 and has a cactus garden out front and a garden sitting area in back with a koi (Japanese carp) pond and spectacular views of the national park rock formations. Rooms are charming, comfortable and quiet, with private bathrooms; they're furnished with an eclectic mixture of contemporary and wicker items, and original art and photography dot the walls. One upstairs room faces west and has grand sunset views, while the other two have private decks facing the impressive formations of Zion. The downstairs suite can accommodate up to five adults.

The gourmet breakfasts are sumptuous yet low fat, and include fresh-baked breads, fresh-squeezed orange juice, granola, fruit, yogurt, and a hot main course that changes daily. Facilities include an outdoor whirlpool.

O'Toole's Bed & Breakfast. 980 Zion Park Blvd. (P.O. Box 29), Springdale, UT 84767. ☎ **435/772-3457.** Fax 435/772-3324. www.otooles.com. 6 units (2 with shared bathroom). A/C. Apr–Oct $69–$79 double; $125 double suite. Lower rates off-season. Rates include full breakfast. DISC, MC, V. Children 8 and older are welcome.

Owners Rick and Michelle O'Toole have furnished this lovely 1929 home with many family antiques, creating an inn that is both attractive and comfortable. On the first floor there are two cheerful rooms, decorated in early-20th-century style. Each has one double bed and a private sink, and they share a bathroom (shower only). Upstairs is the large suite, utilizing the entire 1,100 square feet, with a vaulted ceiling, a wood-burning stove, its own kitchen, and a claw-foot tub in the bathroom. There is a queen bed and queen futon, and views of the gardens and national park. The cute Garden Cottage, which was moved here from inside the national park, contains three rooms. Two small but comfortable rooms, each with one queen-size bed, are on the main floor; plus there's a basement room with a double bed. In the backyard is an attractive garden area with seating and a gas barbecue. Breakfast generally includes home-baked breads, fresh fruit, and a hot main dish such as omelets or pancakes.

⊘ **Snow Family Guest Ranch.** 633 E. Utah 9 (P.O. Box 790190), Virgin, UT 84779. ☎ **800/308-7669** or 435/635-2500. Fax 435/635-2758. www.snowfamilyranch.com. E-mail: bandb@redrock.net. 10 units. A/C. $85–$105 double. Rates include full breakfast. AE, DISC, MC, V.

Nestled in the shadow of Zion National Park on 12 acres of green pastures, all enclosed in white rail fences, this lovely horse ranch is about 12 miles west of the park and about 30 miles east of St. George. Rooms are individually decorated with an elegant western flair, with handsome log furnishings and one or two queen-size beds, a king, or two twins. The large bridal suite has a massive log bed, claw-foot tub, and separate shower. All rooms have private bathrooms, and most have comfortable window seats. Views from the rooms look out across the ranch to the silent red rock mesas and canyons beyond. A full breakfast is served each morning, and light refreshments are offered in the afternoon. Guests share a living room with piano, and a separate TV room with a big-screen TV. There is a swimming pool, hot tub, a gazebo, and a pond. Guided scenic trail rides are offered for an additional charge.

Terrace Brook Lodge. 990 Zion Park Blvd. (P.O. Box 217), Springdale, UT 84767. ☎ **800/342-6779** or 435/772-3932. Fax 435/772-3596. www. terracebrooklodge.com. 27 units. A/C TV. $49–$63 double; $79–$94 suite. AE, DISC, MC, V.

Reasonable rates for clean, well-maintained rooms are what you'll find here, and there's even an outdoor, heated swimming pool. This comfortable, older motel has Southwest decor with light wood furnishings. Four rooms have shower only; the rest have shower/tub combos. There are two barbecue and picnic areas, and bicycle storage is available. During the summer, guided van tours ($49 per person) are offered to Zion Canyon, Bryce Canyon, the north rim of the Grand Canyon, and Lake Powell.

Zion Park Motel. 855 Zion Park Blvd. (P.O. Box 365), Springdale, UT 84767. ☎ **435/772-3251.** 21 units. A/C TV TEL. $59–$66 double, $79–$99 suite. AE, DISC, MC, V.

This economical motel offers comfortable, attractively furnished rooms. All units have either showers or tub/shower combos, and two suites have full kitchens. Facilities include a seasonal outdoor heated pool, picnic area, and playground. A self-service laundry, a small but well-stocked grocery store with camping supplies and an ATM, and a restaurant are adjacent.

WHERE TO DINE

You won't find any stores selling picnic and/or camping provisions inside Zion National Park. However, Springdale has several stores offering a variety of items. See the Fast Facts entry for "Supplies" in chapter 3, "Exploring Zion National Park."

✪ **Bit & Spur Restaurant & Saloon.** 1212 Zion Park Blvd., Springdale. ☎ **435/772-3498.** Reservations recommended. Main courses $7–$16.50. MC, V. Mar–Oct daily 5–10pm (bar open until 1am) and a weekend brunch is offered May–Sept (call for hours); Nov–Feb Thurs–Mon 5–10pm. Closed Christmas holidays. MEXICAN/SOUTHWESTERN.

Rough wood-and-stone walls and an exposed beam ceiling give this restaurant the look of an Old West saloon, but it's an unusually clean saloon that also has a family dining room, patio dining, and original oil paintings on the walls. The food here is also a notch or two above what might be expected, closer to what you'd find in a good Santa Fe restaurant. The menu includes Mexican standards such as burritos, flautas, chile rellenos, and a traditional chile stew with pork and rice; but you'll also find more exotic creations, such as *pollo relleno*—a grilled breast of chicken stuffed with cilantro pesto and goat cheese, and served with pineapple salsa. Also good are the deep-dish chicken enchilada, with scallions, green chiles, and cheese; and the Moroccan spiced lamb—a braised lamb shank with a sweet tamarind glaze, black-eyed pea ragout, and rice. Several vegetarian items are also available. The Bit & Spur has full liquor service and an extensive wine list.

Bumbleberry Restaurant & Gift Shop. 897 Zion Park Blvd., Springdale. ☎ **435/772-3611.** Lunch $4.65–$6.45; dinner $5.45–$17.95. DISC, MC, V. Daily 7am–10pm; shorter hours in winter. AMERICAN.

A coffee shop with comfortable booths along the windows sits in front; a more formal restaurant with a high ceiling and light-colored walls with brick accents sits in back. All the food is made from scratch. Breakfasts include a variety of egg dishes, including a vegetarian omelet, plus Bumbleberry pancakes and French toast. The lunch menu includes the popular fish and chips, sandwiches, and burgers. Dinner entrees include chicken fried steak, barbecued chicken, vegetarian spaghetti, and broiled New York strip steak. The restaurant prides itself on its homemade pies—especially the Bumbleberry Pie, with its secret mix of berries. No alcohol is served.

The restaurant's playhouse hosts live theater each summer; see "Attractions," above.

Flanigan's Inn. 428 Zion Park Blvd., Springdale. ☎ **435/772-3244.** Reservations recommended. Main course grills $8.95–$18. AE, DISC, MC, V. Mon–Thurs 3–9:30pm, Fri–Sun 3–10pm; shorter hours in winter. AMERICAN/REGIONAL.

This restaurant has a greenhouse/garden atmosphere and makes the most of the area's spectacular scenery with large windows for inside diners plus an outdoor patio. Flanigan's uses fresh local ingredients and herbs from the inn's garden whenever possible. The menu includes items such as wood-fired pizzas, pastas, salads, and black Angus beef. Especially recommended are the New York steak in a green peppercorn sauce and the grilled spring lamb chops with a demi glace sauce. Microbrewery draft beers are available, and the wine cellar stocks over 2,000 bottles.

Panda Garden. 805 Zion Park Blvd., Springdale. ☎ **435/772-3535.** Lunch $4.95–$6.95; dinner $7.25–$18.95. AE, DISC, MC, V. Daily noon–11pm. Closed Dec–Feb. CHINESE.

Chinese art, soft music, and green plants create a pleasant ambiance in this large, open room, with 18 tables inside and 14 on the patio. Lunch is served until 3pm and offers a wide variety of items including chow mein (chicken, pork, or beef) and sweet and sour pork or chicken. You can also get hot and spicy choices such as Hunan beef and Yu-shang shrimp. The dinner menu lists more than 50 Chinese dishes, with a dozen seafood choices plus numerous beef and chicken selections. Chef's specials include Triple Delight—gan-shiao spicy shrimp, chicken broccoli, and beef snow peas; and New York steak Chinese style—a 10-ounce steak cooked in a very hot wok with fresh vegetables, all in a rich broth. Beer is served.

Reese's Log House Restaurant. 2400 Zion Park Blvd., Springdale. ☎ **435/ 772-3000.** Reservations not accepted. Main courses lunch $4.95–$8.95, dinner $7.95–$21.95. AE, CB, DC, DISC, MC, V. Daily 11:30am–9pm. AMERICAN.

This magnificent log structure—built with logs salvaged from the great 1988 fire in Yellowstone National Park—boasts splendid views from every window. The casual atmosphere is reflected in the high-beamed ceiling, log walls, simple western decor, solid wood tables, and cushioned chairs. Slate tile from India was used on the floor. There are hot sandwiches for lunch, including the standard burger, plus turkey, chicken breast, fish, and steak; and cold deli sandwiches, soup, pasta, and salads. The dinner menu includes chicken fried steak, a turkey breast tenderloin steak, several beef steaks, and the Log House specialty chicken dinner. Beer and wine are served.

The huge building also houses a gift shop, a desk offering national park information, a western clothing store, and a North American wildlife exhibit—deer, elk, Alaskan brown bear, polar bear, and a variety of fish including a great white shark.

✪ Zion Park Gift & Deli. 666 Zion Park Blvd., Springdale. ☎ **435/ 772-3843.** $4.30–$8.20. AE, DISC, MC, V. Summer, Mon–Sat 8am–9pm; shorter hours in winter. SANDWICHES.

This is a good choice for a top quality deli-style sandwich at an economical price. You can eat at one of the cafe-style tables inside, on the outdoor patio, or carry your sandwich off for a hike or to one of the national park's picnic grounds. All baked goods, including the excellent sandwich breads and sub rolls, are made in-house. In typical fast-food restaurant style, you order at the counter and wait as your meal is prepared with your choice of bread, meats, cheeses, and condiments. It's also a good breakfast stop for those who enjoy fresh-baked cinnamon rolls, muffins, banana nut bread, and similar goodies, with a cup of espresso. Locally made candy and 16 flavors of ice cream and frozen yogurt are also offered. No alcohol is served.

✪ **Zion Pizza & Noodle.** 868 Zion Park Blvd., Springdale. ☎ **435/ 772-3815.** www.zionpizzanoodle.com. Reservations not accepted. Entrees $7.95–$11.95. No credit cards. Summer, Mon–Thurs 4–10:30pm; Fri– Sun 11:30am–10:30pm. Shorter hours in winter. PIZZA/PASTA.

This busy cafe, located in a former church with a turquoise steeple, has small, closely spaced tables and black-and-white photos on the walls. Patrons order at the counter and help themselves at the soft drink beverage bar while waiting for their food to be delivered. The 12-inch pizzas, with lots of chewy crust, are baked in a slate stone oven. They're good, but pizza purists might be put off by oddly topped specialty pies, such as the southwestern burrito pizza or barbecue chicken pizza. But have no fear—you can get a basic cheese pizza or add any of the roughly 15 extra toppings, from pepperoni to green chiles to pineapple. The noodle side of the menu offers a variety of pastas, such as penne pasta with grilled chicken, broccoli, carrots, fresh cream, and cheese; calzones; and stromboli. Take out and delivery are available. The restaurant serves microbrews and domestic beer.

2 East Entrance Gateway to Zion National Park

Although there is no town outside the east entrance to Zion National Park, there are several businesses that provide visitor services. Also see the section for Mt. Carmel Junction (below).

WHERE TO STAY
Room tax is about 10%.

Mukuntuweep RV Park & Campground. About a quarter mile east of the east entrance to Zion National Park on Utah 9 (P.O. Box 193, Orderville, UT 84758). ☎ **435/648-2154.** www.xpressweb.com/zionpark. $25 double; campsites $14–$19. AE, DISC, MC, V.

This attractive compound offers some shade trees, grassy tent sites, a fishing pond, a playground, and a game room, plus great views of the surrounding rocks. There are six basic but comfortable log cabins, a hogan, and a teepee, which share the campground's bath house. Across the street, under the same management, is a store, a restaurant (see "Where to Dine," below), a curio shop, and a gas station.

WHERE TO DINE
There are no stores inside Zion National Park. If you're looking for picnic and camping fodder, there is a small store outside the east entrance to the park. See the Fast Facts entry for "Supplies" in chapter 3, "Exploring Zion National Park."

Zion Mt. Carmel Restaurant. A quarter mile east of the east entrance to Zion National Park (P.O. Box 193, Orderville, UT 84758). ☎ **435/648-2829.** Breakfast $3.25–$5.95; sandwiches $3.50–$5.50; Mexican dishes $2.95–$7.95. AE, DISC, MC, V. Daily 9am–5pm. AMERICAN/MEXICAN.

This down-home coffee shop offers great homemade pies, spicy New Mexico–style Southwest dishes, shakes and sundaes, and burgers and sandwiches. Locals love the green chile beef and bean burrito, and the enchilada-style burrito, which is smothered with chile sauce. The breakfast menu includes the standards: ham and eggs, omelets, pancakes, and French toast. No alcoholic beverages are served.

3 Tropic & Bryce

Just outside the entrance to Bryce Canyon National Park are the communities of Tropic (elevation 6,300 feet and population 400), along Utah 12 about 8 miles east of the park entrance road, and Bryce, along the entrance road and near its intersection with Utah 12. Much of the lodging, dining, and other services for park visitors can be found in these communities.

Tropic was named in 1891 during construction of nearby Tropic Reservoir, when workers said that compared to the nearby town of Panguitch, the climate felt tropical. Bryce, of course, takes its name from the park and its namesake, Ebenezer Bryce.

ESSENTIALS In an **emergency,** dial ☎ **911.** For visitor information, contact the **Garfield County Travel Council,** P.O. Box 200, Panguitch, UT 84759 (☎ **800/444-6689** or 435/676-8826; fax 435/676-8239; www.brycecanyoncountry.com).

OUTDOOR PURSUITS & ATTRACTIONS

There are a variety of outdoor activities in the Dixie National Forest—hiking, mountain biking, fishing, horseback riding, cross-country skiing, and snowshoeing.

Stop at the national forest's **Red Canyon Visitor Center,** (usually open from early May through mid-October) along Utah 12 about 10^1/$_2$ miles west of the Bryce Canyon National Park entrance road (☎ **435/676-2676**); or contact the **Dixie National Forest,** 82 North 100 E., Cedar City, UT 84720 (☎ **435/ 865-3700**). Also see "Dixie National Forest" in chapter 9, "Nearby Things to See & Do."

For other diversions, the **Best Western Ruby's Inn** (☎ **435/ 834-5341**), on Utah 63 just north of the Bryce Canyon National Park entrance (see "Where to Stay," below), is practically a one-stop entertainment center for those looking for a bit of variety in their national park vacation.

Directly across Utah 63 from the motel are **Old Bryce Town Shops,** open from mid-May to September, where you'll find a rock shop, souvenir shops, a Christmas store, and an opportunity to buy that genuine cowboy hat you've been wanting. Next to the shops is a children's petting farm (free admission), with performing horses and a cowboy poet; you can also try your hand at gold panning ($4 pan rental).

Nearby, **Bryce Canyon Country Rodeo** has bucking broncos, bull riding, calf roping, and all sorts of rodeo fun in a 1-hour program from Memorial Day to August, Monday to Saturday evenings at 7:30pm. Admission is $7 for adults and $4 for children under 12.

WHERE TO STAY

Room tax is about 9%. Pets are not accepted unless otherwise noted.

✪ **Best Western Ruby's Inn.** Utah 63 at the entrance to Bryce Canyon (P.O. Box 1), Bryce, UT 84764. ☎ **800/528-1234** or 435/834-5341. Fax 435/834-5265. www.rubysinn.com. 369 units, including 60 suites. A/C TV TEL. June–Sept $90–$115 double; $120–$130 suite. Apr–May and Oct $63–$95 double; $100–$120 suite. Nov–Mar $46–$73 double; $83–85 suite. AE, CB, DC, DISC, MC, V. Pets accepted.

Most of the tired hikers and canyon rim gazers visiting Bryce Canyon National Park stay at this large Best Western. The lobby, with a stone fireplace and a western motif of animal head trophies and American Indian blankets, is among the busiest places in the area. It boasts an ATM, a small liquor store, car rentals, a beauty salon, a 1-hour film processor, and tour desks where you can arrange excursions of all sorts, from horseback and all-terrain-vehicle rides to helicopter flights. Just off the lobby is a restaurant (see "Where to Dine," below); a western art gallery; a huge general store that offers souvenirs, western clothing, camping supplies, and groceries; and a U.S. post office. Outside there are two gas stations.

Spread among nine separate buildings, the modern motel rooms have light-colored walls decorated with art depicting scenes of the area, wood furnishings, and shower/tub combos. Some have whirlpool tubs, including a few that will accommodate two people. Rooms at the back of the complex will be a bit quieter, but you'll have to walk farther to all the lobby activities. Amenities include a concierge, courtesy transportation from the Bryce Airport, two indoor pools, one indoor and one outdoor whirlpool, a sundeck, bicycle rental, nature and cross-country ski trails, a game room, a business center, conference rooms for up to 300, and two coin-operated laundries.

Bryce Canyon Pines. Utah 12 (3 miles west of intersection with park entry road; P.O. Box 43, Bryce, UT 84764). ☎ **800/892-7923** or 435/834-5441. Fax 435/834-5330. www.bcpines@colorcountry.net. 51 units. A/C TV TEL. Summer, $75–$80 double; $95–$115 kitchenettes and suites. Lower rates in winter. AE, CB, DC, DISC, MC, V.

A modern motel with a western flair, the Bryce Canyon Pines offers well-maintained rooms with light-colored wood furnishings, a table and two padded chairs, and two queen-size beds in most rooms. Some units have fireplaces (wood supplied free in winter), some have fully-stocked kitchenettes, and one has its own whirlpool tub. There's a covered, heated swimming pool, and an adjacent restaurant (see "Where to Dine," below). You can also book horseback rides from Red Canyon Trail Rides (see "Dixie National Forest" in chapter 9) and trail ride/lodging packages.

Bryce Canyon Resorts. 13500 E. Utah 12 (P.O. Box 640006), Bryce, UT 84764. ☎ **800/834-0043** or 435/834-5351. Fax 435/834-5256. 50 units. A/C TV TEL. Summer, $69–$85 double; lower rates at other times. DISC, MC, V. Pets accepted for a fee plus deposit.

This complex, which includes a motel, restaurant, and campground, is adjacent to the main parking area for the new Bryce Canyon shuttle at the intersection of Utah 12 and Utah 63. A massive renovation was underway during our visit, but from what had already been completed it appeared that this will be a very attractive property, and a somewhat elegant change-of-pace from the western and southwestern decor found in most other lodgings in the area.

Rooms are Victorian, with drapes and bed coverings in royal purples and reds, and solid wood furniture stained a rich mahogany. Each of the spacious rooms contains one king- or two queen-size beds, a table with two upholstered chairs, two sinks, a shower-tub combo, a TV in an armoire, an ample closet, and better-than-average lighting. There are two suites, one with a fireplace. There is an indoor pool and sauna, and a restaurant, Hoo-Doo's (see "Where to Dine," below).

Bryce Country Cabins. 320 N. Utah 12 (P.O. Box 141), Tropic, UT 84776. ☎ **888/679-8643** or 435/679-8643. Fax 435/679-8989. www.brycecountrycabins.com. 8 units. A/C TV. Summer, $65–$75 double; lower rates rest of year. DC, MC, V.

There are six new log-style cabins and a two-room pioneer cottage on this 20-acre farm along the highway. The grounds surrounding the cabins and cottage are nicely landscaped, and you get views out over the national park, but the intriguing part is the farm behind the buildings, where cattle graze in the fields and the chickens think they own the place.

The comfortable cabins have knotty pine walls and ceilings, exposed beams, and ceiling fans. Each has two queen-size beds, a table with two chairs, a coffeemaker, and a private porch. Sinks are outside the bathrooms, which have showers only. The cottage, built in 1905, has two spacious rooms with country-style decor, each with its own entrance. Both have full bathrooms with shower/tub combos; one room has a king-size bed, while the other has two queens. The two rooms can be rented together or individually. Room telephones for both the cottage and the cabins were planned for 2000.

Bryce Pioneer Village. 80 S. Main St. (Utah 12; P.O. Box 119), Tropic, UT 84776. ☎ **800/222-0381** or 435/679-8546. Fax 435/679-8607. www.bpvillage.com. E-mail: info@bpvillage.com. 69 units. A/C TV TEL. $60–$85 double; $39–$85 cabins. DISC, MC, V. Pets accepted.

This is a good choice for those seeking a good night's rest at a reasonable rate. The small, no-frills motel rooms in a modular building have showers only (no tubs) but they're clean, comfortable, and have fairly large walk-in closets. Cabins, which were relocated from inside the national park, are more interesting. Most are small but cute, with one queen bed plus a twin bed, one chair, and a small bathroom with a corner shower but no tub. Several others, which have been renovated within the past few years, are much larger, with two queen beds, attractive floral-print wallpaper, and average-size bathrooms with shower/tub combinations. There are also two rooms with three queen beds each. There's an indoor heated swimming pool, whirlpool, two hot tubs, a picnic area, and a small curio shop. Just outside the motel office, you can see the cabin where Ebenezer and Mary Bryce, for whom the national park is named, lived in the late 1870s.

☻ Bryce Point Bed & Breakfast. 61 N. 400 W. (P.O. Box 96), Tropic, UT 84776-0096. ☎ **435/679-8629.** 6 units. TV. $70 double; $90–$120 honeymoon cottage. Rates include full breakfast. MC, V.

Lamar and Ethel LeFevre have named and decorated each room in their bed-and-breakfast for one of their children. For instance, son Les is a firefighter, so the Les and Dela room contains fire-fighting memorabilia and photos; and because son Lynn is in the airline industry, you'll find mementos centering on airplanes in Lynn and

Karen's room. The decor is tasteful and not overdone, and most rooms offer beautiful views of Bryce Point through large picture windows. All rooms have queen beds and private bathrooms (showers only); and all have TV/VCR combos, with free use of the LeFevre's video collection. The honeymoon cottage is beautifully furnished in country style, with a gas fireplace in the living room, full kitchen, washer and dryer, and a king bed in the spacious bedroom. Breakfasts are full, satisfying, and homemade, with selections such as bacon and eggs with pancakes and apple cider syrup. All guests have use of a large enclosed hot tub. The B&B is entirely nonsmoking.

Bryce View Lodge. Utah 63 across from Best Western Ruby's Inn (P.O. Box 64002), Bryce, UT 84764. ☎ **888/279-2304** or 435/834-5180. Fax 435/834-5181. www.bryceviewlodge.com. 160 units. A/C TV TEL. $44–$55 double. AE, CB, DC, DISC, MC, V. Pets accepted.

This basic modern American motel consists of four two-story buildings, set back from the road and grouped around a large parking area and the location of the future swimming pool (planned by 2001). Rooms are simple but comfortable, with an occasional western touch, and are pretty quiet. All rooms have the vanity outside the bathroom, and a table and two chairs; most have one or two double beds, some have a queen. Guests have access to the amenities across the street at Ruby's (see above).

Canyon Livery Bed & Breakfast. 50 S. 660 W. (P.O. Box 24), Tropic, UT 84776-0024. ☎ **888/889-8910** or 435/679-8780. Call for fax. www.canyonlivery.com. E-mail: tclbnb@color-country.net. 5 units. A/C. Apr–Oct $75–$95 double; Nov–Mar $65–$75 double. Rates include full breakfast. MC, V.

The simply decorated rooms in this delightful bed-and-breakfast have beautiful handmade quilts on the queen beds. Two are dedicated to women pioneers and have brass beds, two have handmade wooden beds and are dedicated to male pioneers. The fifth is western, with a wonderful high arched window providing terrific views of the night sky. Breakfasts include a hot dish, homemade breads—usually one baked fresh that morning—plus fresh fruits (often from the B&B's own trees), juices, and coffee. All rooms have windows facing the national park, and the three upstairs rooms have private balconies. Each has its own entrance, and there is a corral if you happen to bring your horse ($5 a day extra, plus food). Smoking is not permitted.

Foster's. Utah 12 (mailing address: Star Route, Panguitch, UT 84759), Bryce, UT. ☎ **800/475-4318** or 435/834-5227. Fax 435/834-5304. E-mail: fosters@color-country.net. 52 units. A/C TV TEL. Winter $50 double; summer $60 double. AE, DISC, MC, V.

Clean and economical lodging is the norm at Foster's, located $1^1/2$ miles west of the national park access road turnoff. A modular unit contains small rooms, each with either one queen-size or two double beds, and decorated with posters showing scenery of the area; bathrooms have showers only. Also on the grounds is a restaurant (see "Where to Dine," below) and a grocery store (open 7am to 8pm, closed December and January) with a rather nice bakery.

World Host Bryce Valley Inn. 199 N. Main St. (Utah 12; 8 miles east of the park entrance road), Tropic, UT 84776. ☎ **800/442-1890** or 435/679-8811. Fax 435/679-8846. www.brycevalleyinn.com. E-mail: bvi@color-country.net. 65 units. A/C TV TEL. Apr–Oct $60–$75 double; Nov–Mar $30–$45 double. AE, DISC, MC, V. Pets accepted for a fee.

These simply decorated, basic motel rooms offer a clean, economical choice for park visitors, 8 miles east of the park entrance road. Rooms, all of which have shower/tub combos and light-colored walls, are furnished with either one or two queen beds. There's one suite with two queens and a hide-a-bed. The motel has a 24-hour coin-operated laundry. The Hungry Coyote Restaurant & Saloon (see "Where to Dine," below) serves American and western cuisine. A gift shop on the premises offers a large selection of American Indian arts and crafts, handmade gifts, rocks, and fossils.

WHERE TO DINE

If you need picnic or camping supplies, there is a small general store inside the national park, as well as several stores not far from the park entrance. See the Fast Facts entry for "Supplies" in chapter 5, "Exploring Bryce Canyon National Park."

Bryce Canyon Pines. Utah 12 about 3 miles west of intersection with park entry road. ☎ **435/834-5441.** Sandwiches $3.75–$6.95; full dinners $9.95–$16.50. AE, CB, DC, DISC, MC, V. Daily 6:30am–10pm (may close slightly earlier in spring and fall). Closed Dec–Feb. AMERICAN.

A country cottage-style dining room, with an old wood stove and white eyelet-trimmed curtains, is a good setting for the wholesome American food served here. Especially popular for its traditional breakfasts, the restaurant is also known for its homemade soups and pies. Both sandwiches and full dinners are available at lunch and dinner. Recommended are the hot sandwiches, such as the open-faced turkey with mashed potatoes and gravy; the Utah trout; and the 8-ounce tenderloin steak. Beer and wine are available.

Canyon Diner. Just north of the park entrance on Utah 63, at Ruby's Inn, Bryce. ☎ **435/834-5341.** Reservations not accepted. Individual items $1.50–$4; meals $5–$7.90. AE, DISC, MC, V. Daily 6:30am–10pm. AMERICAN.

Part of the Ruby's Inn complex, this fast-food restaurant is a great place to fill up the kids without going broke. Breakfasts, served until 11am, include several egg croissants; for lunch and dinner, you can get hoagies, burgers, hot dogs, particularly good stuffed potatoes, pizza, fried chicken, and salads. We especially recommend the Piccadilly (English-style) chips. Specialties include the mesquite-smoked half-chicken and a fish-and-chips basket. On a hot day, try a basic salad complemented by a filling malt or milkshake. No alcohol is served.

Foster's Family Steak House. Utah 12 about 1¹/₂ miles west of the park entrance road. ☎ **435/834-5227.** Reservations not accepted. Breakfast and lunch items $1.75–$6; main dinner courses $9–$19. AE, DISC, MC, V. Mar–Nov daily 7am–10pm; Dec–Feb daily 5–10pm. STEAK/SEAFOOD.

The simple western decor here provides the appropriate atmosphere for a family steakhouse, popular among locals for its slow-roasted prime rib and steamed Utah trout. Foster's also offers several steaks, including a 14-ounce T-bone, sandwiches, a soup of the day, and homemade western-style chile with beans. All the pastries, pies, and breads are baked on the premises. Bottled beer is available.

Hoo-Doo's Restaurant. 13500 E. Utah 12, at its intersection with Utah 63 (at Bryce Canyon Resorts). ☎ **435/679-8966.** Lunch $3.95–$6.95; dinner $10.45–$16.95. AE, DISC, MC, V. Daily 6:30am–10pm. Closed mid-Nov to mid-April. STEAK/SEAFOOD.

This family steakhouse, with light wood walls and a decidedly western atmosphere, specializes in innovative twists on American standards, such as a 10-ounce choice sirloin, marinated in a lime sauce and flame broiled; and Cajun-style blackened rainbow trout, pan fried. The dinner menu also includes simply prepared flame-broiled steaks, pan-fried salmon and local trout, chicken, and pork chops. Gourmet pizzas are served in a separate dining room, with a big-screen TV. You'll find traditional American breakfasts—try the pancakes—and burgers and sandwiches at lunch. Beer is available. There's also a Hoo-Doo's Restaurant at Doug's Place, 141 N. Main St., Tropic (☎ **435/679-8633**), which doesn't have pizza, but does offer Texas-style barbecue.

Hungry Coyote Restaurant & Saloon. 199 N. Main St. at the World Host Bryce Valley Inn, Tropic. ☎ **435/679-8822.** Breakfast $3.95–$6.95; dinner $6–$21. AE, DISC, MC, V. Daily 6–11am and 5–11pm; shorter hours in winter. AMERICAN/WESTERN.

Rough wood walls, old ranch tools, kerosene lanterns, and warnings that patrons must "check your gun with the waitress" all contribute to the Old West atmosphere. Beef lovers will savor the thick

20-ounce T-bone, the most expensive item on the menu; also popular is the local trout. Other choices include pork chops and grilled chicken breast. The restaurant offers full liquor service.

Ruby's Inn Cowboy's Buffet and Steak Room. Ruby's Inn complex, Bryce. ☎ **435/834-5341.** Breakfast buffet $7.50 adults, $6 children 3–12; lunch buffet $8.50 adults, $7 children 3–12; main courses breakfast and lunch $3–$13.50; dinner buffet $14.50 adults, $7 children 3–12; main dinner courses $5.50–$19.50. AE, CB, DC, DISC, MC, V. Summer daily 6:30am–9:30pm; winter daily 6:30am–8:30pm. STEAK/SEAFOOD.

The busiest restaurant in the Bryce Canyon area, Ruby's moves 'em through with buffets at every meal plus a well-rounded menu and friendly service. The breakfast buffet offers more choices than the usual family-restaurant buffet, with scrambled eggs, fresh fruit, several breakfast meats, potatoes, pastries, and cereals; and as part of the buffet, you can also get omelets and eggs cooked to order. The lunch buffet serves up country-style ribs, fresh fruit, salads, soups, vegetables, and breads; and the dinner buffet features slow-roasted beef and other meats, pastas, potatoes, and salads. Regular menu dinner entrees include prime rib, breaded-and-grilled southern Utah rainbow trout, broiled chicken breast, burgers, and salads. Full liquor service is available.

4 Mt. Carmel Junction

Located at the junction of Utah 9 and U.S. 89, Mt. Carmel Junction, at an elevation of 5,191 feet, is 13 miles east of the east entrance to Zion National Park, 73 miles southwest of Bryce Canyon National Park, and 17 miles northwest of Kanab.

ESSENTIALS   In an **emergency,** dial ☎ **911** or **435/644-2667.** For area information, contact the **Kane County Visitors Center,** 78 S. 100 East, Kanab, UT 84741 (☎ **800/733-5263** or 435/ 644-5033; fax 435/644-5923; www.kaneutah.com; e-mail: kanetrav@kaneutah.com). The nearest medical facility is **Kane County Hospital and Skilled Nursing Facility,** 220 W. 300 North St., Kanab (☎ **435/644-5811**).

WHERE TO STAY

Room tax is about 10%.

Best Western Thunderbird Resort. At the junction of Utah 9 and U.S. 89 (P.O. Box 5536), Mt. Carmel Junction, UT 84755. ☎ **888/848-6358** or 435/ 648-2203. Fax 435/648-2239. www.bwthunderbird.com. 62 units. A/C TV TEL. Apr–Oct $79 double; $95 suite. Nov–Mar $46 double; $58 suite. Closed Christmas Day. AE, DC, DISC, MC, V. Small pets accepted with prior approval.

A two-story motel with southwestern decor, the Thunderbird offers quiet, spacious, and comfortable rooms, with king or queen beds, wood furnishings, photos or artwork depicting area scenery, and a balcony or patio. There is a large outdoor heated pool, a whirlpool, 9-hole golf course ($8 for 9 holes, $15 for 18), gift shop, convenience store with deli, coin-operated laundry, restaurant (see "Where to Dine," below), and a gas station.

Golden Hills Motel. At the junction of Utah 9 and U.S. 89 (P.O. Box 34), Mt. Carmel Junction, UT 84755. ☎ **800/648-2268** or 435/648-2268. Fax 435/648-2558. www.goldenhillsmotel.com. E-mail: gldnhill@color-country.net. 32 units. A/C TV TEL. May–Oct $43–$46 double; $62–$75 suite. Nov–Apr $28–$34 double; $49–$59 suite. AE, DISC, MC, V. Pets accepted at management's discretion.

Rooms, a number of which have been recently redecorated, are simply and comfortably furnished, and many have lovely views of the East Fork of the Virgin River. Suites and family units are large and especially attractive. There's complimentary coffee and tea in the morning and a gift shop with snacks. There is also a full-service restaurant, a heated outdoor pool, and coin-operated laundry.

WHERE TO DINE

Golden Hills Restaurant. At the junction of Utah 9 and U.S. 89 at the Golden Hills Motel. ☎ **435/648-2602.** Reservations for busses only. Lunch $3.25–$5.25; dinner $6.95–$16.95. MC, V. Summer daily 7am–10pm; winter daily 8am–8pm. AMERICAN.

This is a simply but attractively decorated family-style restaurant, where you'll find made-from-scratch breads, pies, and soups. Breakfasts include the usual egg and pancake offerings; lunch is burgers and sandwiches, a soup and salad bar, plus scones with butter and honey. For dinner you can get steak, chicken, fish, pork, and pasta. Locals love the country-fried steak and cream of broccoli soup.

Thunderbird Restaurant. At the junction of Utah 9 and U.S. 89 in the Best Western. ☎ **435/648-2203.** Reservations not accepted. Lunch $4.35–$7.95; dinner entrees $7.95–$16.95. AE, CD, DC, DISC, MC, V. Summer daily 7am–10pm; winter daily 7am–8pm. Closed Christmas Day.

This spacious restaurant offers both booths and tables in a comfortable, southwestern setting. The decor is simple and attractive, in pastels with wood accents. Pancakes are a popular breakfast choice, though there's also French toast, cereal, fruit, breads, numerous egg dishes, and even a hearty steak and eggs platter. Lunch consists of a wide variety of sandwiches and burgers. Dinner entrees include steak, seafood, and chicken, plus liver and onions, country-fried steak, and the popular pot roast. A soup and salad bar is open at dinner also. Beer and wine are served.

9

Nearby Things to See & Do

*T*he area surrounding Zion and Bryce Canyon National Parks offers a smorgasbord of scenic wonders and recreational opportunities, helping you round out your trip to southern Utah. Within 90 minutes of the south entrance to Zion National Park, you can wander through the mysterious lava caves of Snow Canyon, or strike out off-road in a dune buggy at Coral Pink Sand Dunes State Park—and that's just for starters. Virtually adjacent to Bryce Canyon National Park is Grand Staircase–Escalante—a vast, new, stunning national monument—as well as Dixie National Forest, a popular spot for mountain bikers. Two other state parks, Kodachrome Basin and Escalante, are within 45 to 60 minutes of the national park entrance and provide lovely vistas and quirky pleasures all their own.

1 Cedar Breaks National Monument

85 miles N of the main section of Zion National Park; 56 miles W of Bryce Canyon National Park

A delightful little monument, this is a wonderful place to spend a few hours or even several days gazing down from the rim into the spectacular natural amphitheater, hiking the trails, and camping among the spruce, firs, and wildflowers that blanket the plateau each summer. This natural coliseum, which looks a lot like Bryce Canyon National Park, is more than 2,000 feet deep and over 3 miles across; it's filled with stone spires, arches, and columns shaped by the forces of erosion and painted in ever-changing reds, purples, oranges, and ochres. But why "Cedar Breaks?" Well, the pioneers who came here called such badlands "breaks," and they mistook the juniper trees along the cliff bases for cedars.

JUST THE FACTS

At over 10,000 feet elevation, it's always pleasantly cool at Cedar Breaks. It actually gets downright cold at night, so take a jacket or sweater, even if the temperature is scorching just down the road in St. George. The monument opens for its short summer season only after the snow melts, usually in late May, and closes in

October—unless you happen to have a pair of cross-country skis or a snowmobile, in which case you can visit year-round.

GETTING THERE   From Zion's south entrance, head west on Utah 9, then north on Utah 17 to I-15. Follow the interstate north to exit 57 for Cedar City, and head east on Utah 14 to Utah 148, turn north (left), and follow Utah 148 into the monument. From the Kolob Canyons section of Zion, which is just off exit 40 of I-15, it is only 40 miles to Cedar Breaks.

Cedar Breaks National Monument is 23 miles east of Cedar City, 56 miles west of Bryce Canyon National Park, and 247 miles south of Salt Lake City. If you're coming from Bryce Canyon or other points east, the park is accessible from the town of Panguitch via Utah 143. If you're traveling from the north, take the Parowan exit off I-15 and head south on Utah 143. It's a steep climb from whichever direction you choose, and vehicles prone to vapor lock or loss of power on hills (such as RVs) may have some problems.

INFORMATION & VISITOR CENTER   One mile from the south entrance gate is a small visitor center with exhibits on the geology, flora, and fauna of Cedar Breaks. It's open daily 8am to 6pm from late May to Labor Day, and 9am to 5:30pm from Labor Day until closing, usually in mid-October. You can purchase books and maps there, and rangers can help plan your visit. For advance information, contact the Superintendent, **Cedar Breaks National Monument,** 2390 W. Utah 56, Suite 11, Cedar City, UT 84720 (☎ **435/586-9451;** www.nps.gov/cbr).

FEES & REGULATIONS   Admission is $4 per vehicle or $2 per person on foot, bike, or motorcycle. Camping costs $10 per night.

Regulations are similar to those at most national parks: Leave everything as you found it. Mountain bikes are not allowed on hiking trails. Dogs, which must be leashed at all times, are prohibited on all trails, in the backcountry, and in public buildings.

HEALTH & SAFETY CONCERNS   The high elevation—10,350 feet at the visitor center—is likely to cause shortness of breath and tiredness, and those with heart or respiratory conditions should consult their doctors before making the trip to Cedar Breaks. You should avoid overlooks and other high, exposed areas during thunderstorms; they're often targets for lightning.

RANGER PROGRAMS   During the monument's short summer season, rangers offer nightly campfire talks at the campground; programs on the area's geology at Point Supreme, a viewpoint near the visitor center, daily on the hour from 10am to 5pm; and guided hikes on Saturday and Sunday mornings. A complete schedule is posted at the visitor center and the campground.

EXPLORING CEDAR BREAKS BY CAR

The 5-mile road through Cedar Breaks National Monument offers easy access to the monument's scenic overlooks and trailheads. Allow 30 to 45 minutes to make the drive. Start at the visitor center and nearby **Point Supreme** for a panoramic view of the amphitheater. Then drive north, past the campground and picnic ground turnoff, to **Sunset View** for a closer look at the amphitheater and its colorful canyons. From each of these overlooks, you'll be able to see out across Cedar Valley, over the Antelope and Black mountains, and into the Escalante Desert.

Continue north to **Chessman Ridge Overlook,** so named because the hoodoos directly below this point appear to be massive stone chess pieces. Watch for swallows and swifts soaring among the rock formations. Get back into your car and head north to **Alpine Pond,** a trailhead for a self-guided nature trail (see "Hiking," below) with an abundance of wildflowers. Finally, you'll reach **North View,** which offers perhaps the best look into the amphitheater. The view here is reminiscent of Bryce Canyon's Queen's Garden, with its stately statues frozen in time.

SPORTS & ACTIVITIES

CAMPING   The 30-site campground, **Point Supreme,** just north of the visitor center, is open from June to mid-September, with sites available on a first-come, first-served basis. It's a beautiful high-mountain setting among tall spruce and firs. There are rest rooms, drinking water, picnic tables, grills, and an amphitheater for the ranger's evening campfire programs. There are no showers or RV hookups. Keep in mind that, even in midsummer, temperatures can drop into the 30s at night at this elevation, so bring cool-weather gear.

HIKING   There are no trails from the rim to the bottom of the amphitheater, but the monument has two high-country trails. The fairly easy 2-mile **Alpine Pond Trail** loop leads to a picturesque forest glade and pond surrounded by wildflowers, and through a woodland of bristlecone pines, offering panoramic views of the amphitheater along the way. A trail guide is available at the trailhead.

A Late Summer Bonanza—The Wildflowers of Cedar Breaks

During its brief summer season, Cedar Breaks makes the most of the warmth and moisture with a spectacular wildflower show. The rim comes alive in a blaze of color, and it's truly a sight to behold. The dazzling display begins practically as soon as the snow melts and reaches its peak during late July and August. It's as though the flowers are trying to outshine the colorful rocks below. Watch for mountain bluebells, spring beauty, beard tongue, and fleabane early in the season; those beauties then make way for columbine, larkspur, Indian paintbrush, wild roses, and other varieties.

A somewhat more challenging hike, the 4-mile **Spectra Point Trail** (also called the Ramparts Trail) follows the rim more closely than the Alpine Pond Trail, offering changing views of the colorful rock formations. It also takes you through fields of wildflowers and by bristlecone pines more than 1,500 years old. You'll need to be especially careful of your footing along the exposed cliff edges, and allow yourself some time to rest—there are lots of ups and downs along the way.

WILDLIFE WATCHING   Because of its relative remoteness, Cedar Breaks is a good place for spotting wildlife. You're likely to see mule deer grazing in the meadows along the road early and late in the day. Marmots make their dens near the rim and are often seen along the Spectra Point Trail; and you'll spot ground squirrels, red squirrels, and chipmunks almost everywhere. Pikas, which are related to rabbits, are here too, but it's unlikely you'll see one—they're small, with short ears and stubby tails, and prefer the high, rocky slopes.

Birders should have no trouble spotting the Clark's nutcracker in the campground, with its gray torso and black-and-white wings and tail. The monument is also home to swallows, swifts, blue grouse, and golden eagles.

WINTER SPORTS & ACTIVITIES   The monument essentially shuts down from late October to mid-May because of the blanket of deep snow that covers it. Snow-blocked roads will keep cars out, but they're perfect for snowmobilers and cross-country skiers, who usually come over from nearby Brian Head ski area. Keep in mind, though, that all facilities are closed and the only people you're likely to see will be an occasional park ranger, patrolling on a snowmobile.

2 Snow Canyon State Park

11 miles NW of St. George; about 60 miles W of Zion National Park

Among Utah's most scenic state parks—sometimes called a "vest pocket Zion"—Snow Canyon offers an abundance of opportunities for photography, hiking, rock climbing, and horseback riding. The park is surrounded by rock cliffs and high walls of Navajo sandstone in every shade of red imaginable, layered with white and black from ancient lava flows. Hike the trails and discover shifting sand dunes, mysterious lava caves, colorful desert plants, and a variety of rock formations. There's also an attractive cactus garden, whose plants are described in a brochure, and several ancient petroglyphs (ask park rangers for directions). By the way, don't come looking for snow—Snow Canyon was named for pioneers Lorenzo and Erastus Snow, who discovered it.

JUST THE FACTS

Because the summers here are hot—well over 100°F—the best time to visit is any other time. Winters are mild, but nights can be chilly. Spring and fall are usually perfect weatherwise, and are therefore the busiest.

GETTING THERE   From Zion National Park, follow Utah 9 to I-15, exit 16; head south to St. George (exit 8); take Utah 18 northwest to the entrance road to the park.

INFORMATION, FEES & REGULATIONS   For a copy of the park's brochure, contact **Snow Canyon State Park Headquarters,** P.O. Box 140, Santa Clara, UT 84765-0140 (☎ **435/628-2255**). Day-use fee is $4 per vehicle or $2 per person on foot, bike, or motorcycle. Like most of Utah's state parks, dogs are welcome, including on the trails, but must be leashed.

CAMPING   Campsites with electricity cost $15, and those without hookups are $13. Reservations are recommended from February to May and September to November; call ☎ **800/322-3770.** There's a $6.25 nonrefundable reservation fee.

The 36-site campground is one of the best in the state park system. One section has electric hookups, but these sites are a bit close together; people not needing electricity can set up camp in delightful little side canyons, surrounded by colorful red rocks and Utah juniper. The views are spectacular no matter where you choose to set up. There are hot showers, modern rest rooms, and an RV sewage dump station.

SPORTS & ACTIVITIES

HIKING   The best way to see Snow Canyon is on foot or horseback (see below). Several short trails make for easy full- or half-day hikes. The **Hidden Piñon Trail** is a $1^1/_2$-mile round-trip self-guided nature trail that wanders among lava rocks, through several canyons, and onto rocky flatlands, offering panoramic views of the surrounding mountains. The trail begins across the highway from the campground; you can pick up a brochure at the park office/entrance station. The walk is fairly easy, but allow at least an hour, especially if you're planning to keep an eye out for Mormon tea, cliffrose, prickly pear cactus, and banana yucca.

An easy three-quarter-mile (one-way) trail leads to **Johnson Arch.** It begins just south of the campground, passes by the popular rock-climbing wall (see below), some low sand dunes, and then a small canyon with a view of Johnson Arch (named after pioneer wife Maude Johnson) high above.

Also popular is the **Lava Caves Trail,** a $1^1/_2$-mile round-trip hike that starts just north of the campground. The caves are about a half mile along the trail, but watch carefully—it's easy to miss them. The caves were formed from liquid lava, and at times American Indian tribes have occupied their large rooms. Another quarter mile past the caves is the West Canyon Overlook, with a breathtaking view into West Canyon.

Several longer and steeper trails lead to spectacular views of the canyons and distant vistas; check with park rangers.

HORSEBACK RIDING   **Snow Canyon Stables,** P.O. Box 577, Santa Clara, UT 84765 (☎ **435/628-6677**), offers year-round horseback rides of various lengths into some of the more inaccessible and beautiful parts of the park. Prices start at $15 for a 1-hour ride; an overnight camping trip, including dinner and breakfast, is $125.

MOUNTAIN BIKING   Although bicycling is not allowed on the park trails, West Canyon Road is open to mountain biking. It lies just west of the park and is 7 miles round-trip. Ask park rangers for directions.

ROCK CLIMBING   Snow Canyon State Park is a popular destination for rock climbers, especially climbers who want to polish their skills a bit before tackling the "experts only" rock walls of Zion National Park. Climbers especially like the tall wall of rock on the east side of the road just south of the campground, but it has become so popular that the park has issued a moratorium on bolting. Check with the park office for information.

WILDLIFE WATCHING　You're likely to see cottontail rabbits, ground squirrels, and songbirds; luckier visitors may also spot desert mule deer, bobcats, coyote, kit foxes, eagles, and owls. Although it's unlikely you'll see one, desert tortoises (a federally listed threatened species) and Gila monsters also live in the park. There are also some rattlesnakes, which you'll want to avoid.

3　Coral Pink Sand Dunes State Park

About 45 miles SE of Zion National Park

Long a favorite for dune buggy enthusiasts (off-road–vehicle users lobbied hard to have this designated a state park), Coral Pink Sand Dunes has recently been attracting an increasing number of campers, hikers, photographers, and all-around nature-lovers as well.

While Big Boys—and occasionally Big Girls—play with their expensive motorized toys, others hike; watch for wildflowers, scorpions, and lizards; or just sit and wiggle their toes in the smooth, cool sand. The colors are especially rich at sunrise and sunset. Early-morning visitors to the dunes will find the tracks of yesterday's dune buggies gone, replaced by the tracks of lizards, kangaroo rats, snakes, and the rest of the park's animal kingdom, who venture out in the coolness of night once all the people have departed.

JUST THE FACTS

At about 5,800 feet elevation, the park gets warm in summer, with temperatures easily reaching the mid 90s, and winters are usually relatively mild, although snow and bitter cold temperatures are not unheard of. Our choice for a visit is May, June, September, and October, when it's delightfully cool at night but warm enough during the day to enjoy burying your toes in the cooling sand. And there are also fewer people there at those times.

GETTING THERE　From Zion National Park, take Utah 9 east to U.S. 89, turn right (south) and continue to the park entrance road. From downtown Kanab, go about 8 miles north on U.S. 89, then southwest (left) on Hancock Road for about 12 miles to get to the park.

INFORMATION & VISITOR CENTER　For copies of the park brochure and off-highway–vehicle regulations, contact the **park office** at P.O. Box 95, Kanab, UT 84741-0095 (☎ **435/648-2800**). At the **park entry station,** there's a small display area with sand from around the world, fossils of the area, and live scorpions, lizards, and tadpoles. The entry station is usually open daily 8am to 9pm, although may be closed briefly while rangers are on patrol.

FEES & REGULATIONS   The day-use fee is $4 per vehicle for up to eight people or $2 per person on foot, bike, or motorcycle.

The standard state park regulations apply here, plus a few extra because of the park's popularity with off-road vehicle users: Quiet hours last from 10pm to 9am, a bit later in the morning than in most parks. The dunes are open to hikers anytime, but to motor vehicles only between 9am and 10pm. Vehicles going onto the dunes must have safety flags, available at the entry station; and vehicles on the dunes must stay at least 10 feet from vegetation and at least 100 feet from hikers. Dogs are permitted on the dunes, but must be leashed.

CAMPING   Camping costs $13. Call ☎ **800/322-3770** for reservations, for an additional $6.25 (nonrefundable) reservation fee per site. The spacious and mostly shady 22-site campground is open all year. There are hot showers, modern rest rooms, and an RV dump station, but no hookups.

RANGER PROGRAMS   Regularly scheduled ranger talks explain the geology, plants, and animals of the dunes. For a real thrill, take a guided evening **Scorpion Walk,** using a black light to find luminescent scorpions that make the park their home. You'll definitely want to wear shoes for this activity! Call to find out if there's one scheduled at the time you'll be there.

SPORTS & ACTIVITIES

HIKING   The best time for hiking the dunes is early morning, for several reasons: It's cooler; the lighting at and just after sunrise produces mysterious shadows and magnificent colors; and there are no noisy dune buggies until after 9am. Sunset is also pretty, but you'll be sharing the dunes with off-road vehicles. Keep in mind that hiking through fine sand can be very tiring, especially for those of us who insist on hiking barefoot. A self-guided half-mile loop nature trail has numbered signs through some of the dunes; allow a half hour for it. Several other good hikes of various lengths are possible within and just outside the park, but because there are few signs and landmarks change with the shifting sands, it's best to check with park rangers before setting out. Those spending more than a few hours in the dunes will discover that even their own tracks disappear in the wind, leaving few clues to the route back to park headquarters.

OFF-ROADING   This giant 1,000-acre sandbox offers plenty of space for off-road–vehicle enthusiasts, who can race up and down the dunes, stopping to perch on a crest to watch the setting sun.

Because the sand here is quite fine, extra-wide flotation tires are needed, and lightweight dune buggies are usually the vehicle of choice. Adjacent to the park, there are hundreds of miles of trails and roads for off-highway–vehicles on Bureau of Land Management property.

4 Grand Staircase–Escalante National Monument

Covering just under 2 million acres, this vast area of red-orange canyons, mesas, plateaus, and river valleys became a national monument by presidential proclamation on September 18, 1996. Known for its stark, rugged beauty, it contains a unique combination of geological, biological, paleontological, archaeological, and historical resources. In announcing the creation of the monument, Pres. Bill Clinton proclaimed, "This high, rugged, and remote region was the last place in the continental United States to be mapped; even today, this unspoiled natural area remains a frontier, a quality that greatly enhances the monument's value for scientific study." The monument bounds up against the Dixie National Forest along Bryce Canyon's east side, so it's little more than a stone's throw from the national park—though getting into the monument can be a bit tricky (see below).

Under the jurisdiction of the Bureau of Land Management, parts of the monument are expected to remain open for grazing and possible oil and gas drilling under existing leases (although no new leases will be issued), as well as hunting, fishing, hiking, camping, and other forms of recreation. A 3-year study was begun immediately, and a management plan is expected to be completed by late 1999.

Unlike most other national monuments, virtually all of this vast area is undeveloped—there are few all-weather roads, only one maintained hiking trail, and two small campgrounds. But for the adventurous, there are miles upon miles of dirt roads and practically unlimited opportunities for hiking, horseback riding, mountain biking on existing dirt roads, and camping.

The national monument can be divided into three distinct sections. The southwest part is the Grand Staircase of sandstone cliffs that includes five life zones ranging from the Sonoran Desert to coniferous forests. The center section is the Kaiparowits Plateau, a vast, wild region of rugged mesas and steep canyons. Finally, along the northern edge of the monument is the Escalante River Canyons section, a delightfully scenic area containing miles of interconnecting river canyons.

Grand Staircase–Escalante National Monument

JUST THE FACTS

Covering such as vast area, weather conditions vary greatly, but it's safe to say that summers are hot. As with most parts of southern Utah, spring and fall are the best times to visit.

GETTING THERE The national monument takes in a large section of southern Utah—covering an area almost as big as the states of Delaware and Rhode Island combined—with Bryce Canyon National Park to the west, Capitol Reef National Park on its northwest edge, and Glen Canyon National Recreation Area along the east and part of the south sides.

Access to the monument is achieved via Utah 12, from Kodachrome Basin State Park (about 22 miles southeast of the Bryce Canyon National Park entrance), and from the town of Escalante (about 50 miles east of Bryce Canyon). You can also reach the Grand Staircase–Escalante via U.S. 89 east of the town of Kanab, which is roughly 80 miles south of Bryce Canyon.

INFORMATION & VISITOR CENTERS   Contact the **Escalante Interagency Office** on the west side of Escalante at 755 W. Main St. (Utah 12), P.O. Box 246, Escalante, UT 84726 (☎ 435/826-5499); or the **Bureau of Land Management/Monument Office** at 318 N. 100 East St., Kanab, UT 84741 (☎ 435/644-2672). These offices offer maps and handouts on a variety of activities. Information is also available on the Web at www.ut.blm.gov/monument. Hours at the Escalante office from mid-March through October are 7:30am to 5:30pm daily; while the rest of the year it's open Monday through Friday from 8am to 4:30pm. The Kanab office is open Monday through Friday from 7:45am to 4:30pm year-round.

FEES, REGULATIONS & SAFETY   There is no charge to enter the monument. Those planning overnight trips into the backcountry should obtain permits (free at this writing) at either of the offices listed above. Regulations are similar to those on other public lands and particularly forbid damaging or disturbing archaeological and historic sites in any way. Dogs are permitted on hiking trails, but should be leashed.

Water is the main safety concern here, either too little or too much. This is generally very dry country, so those going into the monument should carry plenty of drinking water. However, thunderstorms can turn the monument's dirt roads into impassable mud bogs in minutes, stranding motorists; and potentially fatal flash floods through narrow canyons can catch hikers by surprise. Everyone planning trips into the monument should check first with one of the offices listed above on current and anticipated weather and travel conditions, and you should be alert to changing conditions as you explore the area.

CAMPING   Backcountry camping is permitted in most areas of the monument with a permit (free at this writing), available at the Escalante and Kanab offices. There are also two drive-in campgrounds.

Calf Creek Recreation Area, about 15 miles northeast of the town of Escalante via Utah 12, has about a dozen sites and a picnic area. Open year-round, the tree-shaded campground is in a scenic, steep canyon along Calf Creek, surrounded by high rock walls. During summer it is often full by 10am. There is a volleyball court and an interpretative hiking trail. The campground has flush toilets and drinking water, but no showers, RV hookups, dump station, or garbage removal. From November through March, water is turned off and only vault toilets are available. Vehicles must ford a shallow creek, and the campground is not recommended for vehicles over 25 feet long. Campsites cost $7 per night; day use costs $2 per vehicle.

The national monument's other drive-in campground is **Deer Creek,** located 6 miles east of the town of Boulder along the scenic Burr Trail Road. There are four primitive sites, no drinking water or other facilities, and camping is free.

SPORTS & ACTIVITIES

HIKING, MOUNTAIN BIKING & HORSEBACK RIDING

At this writing, the national monument has only one maintained hiking trail. Located about 15 miles northeast of Escalante via Utah 12, the **Calf Creek Recreation Area** has a campground (see "Camping," above), a picnic area with fire grates and tables, trees, drinking water, and flush toilets. The tree-shaded picnic and camping area lies along the creek at the bottom of a high-walled, rather narrow rock canyon. The best part of the recreation area, though, is the moderately strenuous $5^{1}/_{2}$-mile round-trip hike to **Lower Calf Creek Falls.** A sandy trail leads along **Calf Creek,** past beaver ponds and wetlands, to a beautiful waterfall, cascading 126 feet down a rock wall into a tree-shaded pool. You can pick up an interpretive brochure at the trailhead.

Even though the Calf Creek Trail is the monument's only officially marked and maintained trail, there are numerous unmarked cross-country routes that are ideal for hiking, mountain biking (on existing dirt roads only), and horseback riding. It is strongly recommended that hikers stop at the Interagency Office in Escalante or the BLM office in Kanab to get recommendations on hiking routes, and to purchase topographic maps. Hikers need to remember that this is wild country, and it can be hazardous. Rangers recommend carrying at least 1 gallon of water per person per day, and warn that all water from streams should be treated before drinking. The potential for flooding is high, and hikers should check with the BLM before attempting to hike through the monument's narrow slot canyons, where they would have no escape during a flash flood. Other hazards include poison ivy in the wetter areas, and poisonous snakes and scorpions. Slickrock, as the name suggests, is slippery, so hikers should wear sturdy hiking boots with good traction soles.

Among popular and relatively easy-to-follow hiking routes is the footpath to **Escalante Natural Bridge,** which repeatedly crosses the river, so be prepared to get wet up to your knees occasionally.

The easy 2-mile (one-way) hike begins at a parking area at the bridge that crosses the Escalante River near Calf Creek Recreation Area, 15 miles northeast of the town of Escalante. From the parking area, hike upstream to Escalante Natural Bridge, on the south side of the river. The bridge is 130 feet high and spans 100 feet. From here you can continue upstream, exploring its side canyons, or turn around and head back to the parking lot.

Also starting at the Utah 12 bridge parking area is a hike downstream to **Phipps Wash.** Mostly moderate, this hike goes about 1¹/₂ miles to the mouth of Phipps Wash, which enters the river from the west. You'll find Maverick Natural Bridge in a north-side drainage of Phipps Wash, and climbing up the drainage on the south side leads to Phipps Arch.

Hiking the national monument's **slot canyons** is very popular, but it can't be stressed too strongly that you need to check on flood potentials before starting out. A sudden rainstorm can cause a flash flood through a narrow canyon miles away, trapping hikers. One challenging and very strenuous slot canyon hike is through **Peek-a-boo and Spooky Canyons,** which are accessed from the Hole-in-the-Rock Scenic Backway (see "Sightseeing & Four-Wheeling," below). Stop at the Escalante Interagency Office for precise directions.

SIGHTSEEING & FOUR-WHEELING   Since this is one of America's least-developed large sections of public land, it offers a wonderful opportunity for exploration by the adventurous. Be aware, though, that roads inside the monument are dirt that turns into mud—and becomes impassable—when it rains.

One particularly popular road is the **Hole-in-the-Rock Scenic Backway,** which is partly in the national monument and partly in the adjacent Glen Canyon National Recreation Area. Like most roads in the monument, this should be attempted in dry weather only. Starting about 5 miles northeast of Escalante off Utah 12, this clearly marked dirt road travels 57 miles (one-way) to the Hole-in-the-Rock, where Mormon settlers in 1880 cut a passage through solid rock to get their wagons down a 1,200-foot drop to the canyon floor and Colorado River below. About 12 miles in, the road passes by the sign to **Devil's Rock Garden,** an area of classic red rock formations and arches, where you'll also find a picnic area (about 1 mile off the main road). The road continues across a plateau of typical desert terrain, ending at a spectacular scenic overlook of Lake Powell. The first 35 miles of the scenic byway are relatively easy (in dry weather) in a standard passenger car, then it gets a bit

These cliffs are bold escarpments hundreds and thousands of feet in altitude—grand steps by which the region is terraced.

—Maj. John Wesley Powell (1880)

steeper and sandier, and the last 6 miles of the road require a high clearance 4-by-4 vehicle. Allow about 6 hours round-trip, and make sure you have plenty of fuel and water.

Another recommended drive in the national monument is the **Cottonwood Canyon Road,** which runs from Kodachrome State Park south to U.S. 89, along the monument's southern edge, a distance of about 46 miles. The road is sandy and narrow, and washboard in places, but is usually passable for passenger cars in dry weather. It mostly follows Cottonwood Wash, with good views of red rock formations plus distant panoramas from hilltops. Unfortunately, views through the canyon are marred by two power lines, which make photography a challenge. About 10 miles east of Kodachrome Basin State Park is a short side road to **Grosvenor Arch.** This magnificent natural stone arch, with an opening 99 feet wide, was named for National Geographic Society founder and editor Gilbert H. Grosvenor, and is well worth the trip.

WILDLIFE VIEWING & BIRD WATCHING   This isolated and rugged terrain offers good habitat for a number of species, including desert bighorn sheep and mountain lions. Over 200 species of birds have been seen, including bald eagles, golden eagles, Swainson's hawks, and peregrine falcons. The best areas for seeing wildlife are along the Escalante and Paria rivers and Johnson Creek.

5 Dixie National Forest

Adjacent to Bryce Canyon National Park

The Dixie National Forest wraps around two-thirds of Bryce Canyon National Park: all down the west side, around the south end, and about halfway up of the east side. There are a variety of outdoor activities in the forest—hiking, mountain biking, fishing, camping, and cross-country skiing—and one national park trail (Sheep Creek Trail) connects with trails in the national forest. The climate and seasons here are similar to Bryce Canyon National Park (see chapter 2).

JUST THE FACTS

INFORMATION & VISITOR CENTER   Stop at the national forest's **Red Canyon Visitor Center,** (usually open from early May through mid-October) along Utah 12 about 10½ miles west of the Bryce Canyon National Park entrance road (☎ **435/676-2676**); or contact the **Dixie National Forest,** 82 North 100 E., Cedar City, UT 84720 (☎ **435/865-3700**). The visitor center is open daily from 8am to 6pm.

CAMPING   King's Creek Campground, above Tropic Reservoir, has graded gravel roads and sites nestled among tall ponderosa pines. About 9½ miles west of the park is **Red Canyon Campground,** named for its vermilion-colored rock formations. See listings under "Camping Near Bryce Canyon National Park," in chapter 7, "Where to Stay & Eat in the Parks."

SPORTS & ACTIVITIES

FISHING   The closest fishing hole to Bryce Canyon National Park is at **Tropic Reservoir,** a large lake in a ponderosa pine forest. From the national park entrance road, drive west about 3 miles on Utah 12, to a gravel road, turn left (south), and go about 7 miles. There is a forest service campground open in the summer, a boat ramp, and fishing for rainbow, brook, and cutthroat trout. Locals say fishing is sometimes better in streams above the lake than in the reservoir itself.

HIKING   There are about a dozen trails in Red Canyon, and a free map is available at forest service offices. Some are open to hikers only; others are open also to mountain bikers, equestrians, and those with all-terrain–vehicles. One especially scenic multiuse trail is the 5.3-mile (one-way) **Casto Canyon Trail,** which runs along the bottom of Casto Canyon. It connects with the 8.7-mile (one-way) **Cassidy Trail** and 3-mile (one-way) **Losee Canyon Trail** to produce a 17-mile loop that is ideal for a backpacking trip of several days. Watch for elk in the winter, and pronghorn antelope and raptors year-round. The Casto Canyon and Losee Canyon trails are considered moderate, while Cassidy Trail ranges from easy to strenuous. See also "Sheep Creek Trail" in chapter 6, "Hikes & Other Outdoor Pursuits in Bryce Canyon National Park."

For a quick walk, take the half-mile **Pink Ledges Trail,** which is actually a series of short trails that starts just outside the Red Canyon Visitor Center. Rated moderate because of a few steep inclines, the trail has several signs discussing trees and plants, and good views of surrounding hoodoos. The only downside is that you can't escape the road noise from Utah 12.

HORSEBACK RIDING   While those who thought to bring their horses have a number of opportunities on the forest's multiuse trails, those without horses of their own can still explore the canyon on horseback with **Red Canyon Trail Rides** (☎ **800/892-7923** or 435/834-5441), with offices at Bryce Canyon Pines Motel (see "Where to Stay" for Tropic & Bryce in chapter 8, "Gateway Towns"). Trail rides are offered from May through October, with rates of $15 for 1 hour, $25 for 2 hours, $35 for a half day, and $85 for a full day, which includes lunch.

MOUNTAIN BIKING   There are numerous opportunities for mountain biking in the national forest, but only on existing roads. A particularly popular route is **Dave's Hollow Trail,** which starts at the Bryce Canyon National Park boundary sign on Utah 63, the park entrance road, about 1 mile south of Ruby's Inn. The double-track trail goes west for about a half mile before connecting with Forest Road 090, where you turn south and ride for about three-quarters of a mile before turning right onto an easy ride through Dave's Hollow to the Dave's Hollow Forest Service Station on Forest Road 087. From here you can retrace your route for an 8-mile round-trip ride; for a longer 12-mile loop, turn right on Forest Road 087 to Utah 12 and then right again back to Utah 63 and the starting point. A third option is to turn left on Forest Road 087 and follow it to Tropic Reservoir (see "Fishing," above).

The **Casto Canyon Trail,** in Red Canyon, is an especially scenic trail open to hikers, mountain bikers, and those on horseback (see "Hiking," above).

Mountain bikes can be rented across the street from **Best Western Ruby's Inn** (☎ **435/834-5341;** see "Where to Stay" for Tropic & Bryce in chapter 8, "Gateway Towns") for $5 an hour, $15 for up to 4 hours, or $25 for a full day. Repairs are also available.

WINTER ACTIVITIES   Cross-country skiing and snowshoeing opportunities abound along trails and old roads in the national forest, and snowmobiling is also popular. Best Western Ruby's Inn (see "Where to Stay" for Tropic & Bryce in chapter 8, "Gateway Towns") grooms over 30 miles (50 kilometers) of ski trails and also rents cross-country ski equipment.

6 Kodachrome Basin State Park

About 22 miles E of the entrance to Bryce Canyon National Park

Kodachrome Basin lives up to its name; its wonderful scenery practically cries out to be captured on film (regardless of brand or type). Named by the National Geographic Society in 1949, the park is chockfull of tall stone "chimneys" and pink-and-white sandstone cliffs, all set among the contrasting greens of sagebrush and piñon and juniper trees. It also abuts and makes a good base for exploring the new Grand Staircase–Escalante National Monument (see above).

JUST THE FACTS

Because temperatures get a bit warm here during the summer—the park is at 5,800 feet elevation—the best times to visit, especially for hikers, are the months of May, September, and October, when there are also fewer people.

GETTING THERE   From Bryce Canyon National Park, go 3 miles north to Utah 12, turn east (right) and go about 12 miles to Cannonville, turn south (right) onto the park's access road (there's a sign), and go about 7 miles to the park entrance.

INFORMATION, FEES & REGULATIONS   Contact the **park office** at P.O. Box 238, Cannonville, UT 84718 (☎ **435/ 679-8562**) for a color brochure and answers to questions about park facilities and services. The day-use fee is $4 per vehicle or $2 each for those entering the park by foot, bicycle, or motorcycle. Camping costs $13. Dogs are permitted in the park and on trails, but must be kept on leashes no more than 6 feet long.

CAMPING   The campground is laid out among the stone chimneys and scattered piñon and juniper trees. See listing under "Camping Near Bryce Canyon National Park," in chapter 7, "Where to Stay & Eat in the Parks."

SPORTS & ACTIVITIES

HIKING   Kodachrome Basin offers several hiking possibilities. Starting just south of the campground, the **Panorama Trail** is moderately difficult, with no steep climbs. At first it follows an old relatively flat wagon route, then climbs to offer views of the park's rock formations before reaching the well-named Panorama Point. Along the way are several possible side-trips, including a short walk to the **Hat Shop,** so named because the formations resemble broad-brimmed hats; and **White Buffalo Loop,** where you should try to spot a formation that looks like—guess what?—a white buffalo. A side-trip on **Big Bear Geyser Trail** is a bit more difficult, winding past Big Bear and Mama Bear rock formations before returning to Panorama Trail. Allow 2 to 3 hours for the Panorama Trail, and an extra hour for Big Bear Geyser Trail.

Fans of arches will want to drive the dirt road to the trailhead for a half-mile round-trip hike to **Shakespeare Arch,** discovered by Park Manager Tom Shakespeare. This trail also has views of a large chimney rock formation.

HORSEBACK RIDING & STAGECOACH RIDES   In the park, **Trail Head Station** (☎ 435/679-8536) offers guided horseback or horse-drawn stagecoach rides. Call for rates and seasons.

WILDLIFE WATCHING   Jackrabbits and chukar partridges are probably the most commonly seen wildlife in the park, although you'll also hear the piñon jay, and you might see an occasional coyote or rattlesnake.

7   Escalante State Park

48 miles E of Bryce Canyon National Park

Large chunks of colorful petrified wood decorate this unique park, which offers hiking, fishing, boating, camping, and panoramic vistas of the surrounding countryside. There's wildlife to watch, trails to hike, and a 30-acre reservoir for boating, fishing, and somewhat chilly swimming.

JUST THE FACTS

The park is open all year, but spring through fall are the best times to visit. Hikers should be prepared for hot summer temperatures and carry plenty of water, though.

GETTING THERE   The park is located about 2 miles southwest of the town of Escalante on Utah 12 at Wide Hollow Road.

INFORMATION & VISITOR CENTER   For a copy of the park brochure, contact **Escalante State Park,** P.O. Box 350, Escalante, UT 84726-0350 (☎ 435/826-4466). The visitor center has displays of petrified wood, dinosaur bones, and fossils, plus an exhibit explaining how petrified wood is formed.

FEES & REGULATIONS   Admission costs $4 per vehicle for day use or $2 for those entering the park by foot, bicycle, or motorcycle. Camping costs $13. Camping reservations (☎ 800/322-3770) are available for a $6.25 nonrefundable fee.

Rock or Wood—What Is This Stuff?

It looks like a weathered, multicolored tree limb, shining and sparkling in the light—but it's heavy, hard, and solid as a rock. Just what is this stuff? It's petrified wood.

Back in the old days—some 135 to 155 million years ago—southern Utah was not at all the way it is today. It was closer to the equator than it is now, which made it a wet, hot land, with lots of ferns, palm trees, and conifers that provided lunch for the neighborhood dinosaurs.

Occasionally, floods would uproot trees, dumping them in flood plains and along sandbars, then burying them with mud and silt. If this happened quickly, the layers of mud and silt would cut off the oxygen supply, halting the process of decomposition—effectively preserving the tree trunks intact.

Later, volcanic ash covered the area, and groundwater rich in silicon dioxide and other chemicals and minerals made its way down to the ancient trees. With the silicon dioxide acting as a glue, the cells of the wood mineralized. Other waterborne minerals produced the colors: Iron painted the tree trunks in reds, browns, and yellows; manganese produced purples and blues in the preserved wood.

Sometime afterward, uplifts from within the earth, along with various forms of erosion, brought the now-petrified wood to the surface (in places like Escalante State Park and the Grand Staircase–Escalante National Monument), breaking it into the shapes we see today—a mere hundred million years or so after the trees were first uprooted.

As at most state parks, regulations are generally common sense and courtesy: Don't damage anything, drive slowly on park roads, and observe quiet hours between 10pm and 7am. In addition, you're asked to resist the temptation to carry off samples of petrified wood. Pets are welcome, even on trails, but must be restrained on leashes no more than 6 feet long.

CAMPING The 22-unit campground, within easy walking distance of the park's hiking trails and reservoir, is open all year. It has hot showers, modern rest rooms, and drinking water, but no RV hookups.

SPORTS & ACTIVITIES

FISHING & BOATING   **Wide Hollow Reservoir,** located partially inside the park, has a boat ramp (though no rentals are available either in the park or in the town of Escalante). The reservoir is a popular fishing hole for rainbow trout and bluegill. There's ice fishing in the winter.

HIKING   The 1-mile self-guided **Petrified Forest Trail** is a moderately strenuous hike among colorful rocks, through a forest of stunted juniper and piñon pine, and past a painted desert, to a field of colorful petrified wood. The hike also offers panoramic vistas of the town of Escalante and surrounding stair-step plateaus. A free brochure is available at the visitor center. Allow about 45 minutes for the walk.

An optional quarter-mile loop off the main trail leads through more petrified wood, but is considerably steeper than the main trail.

WILDLIFE & BIRD WATCHING   This is one of the best spots in this part of the state to see waterbirds; the reservoir is home to ducks, geese, and coots. Chukar partridges wander throughout the park, and you're also likely to see eagles, hawks, lizards, ground squirrels, and both cottontails and jackrabbits. Binoculars are helpful.

10

A Nature Guide to Zion & Bryce Canyon National Parks

*M*agnificently diverse, Zion and Bryce Canyon National Parks contain burning deserts, lush woodlands with shimmering ponds, barren, windswept ledges of solid rock, and deep forests of pine and fir. These habitats, with their variety of terrain and climates, support a wide range of plants and animals, in a diversity that is primarily the result of elevation and availability of water. Zion, ranging from 3,700 feet to 8,726 feet above sea level, has a larger variety of plants and animals than cooler and higher Bryce Canyon, with elevations from 6,620 feet to 9,115 feet.

1 Zion & Bryce Canyon National Parks Today

While much of southern Utah is barren and sometimes drab desert, Zion and Bryce Canyon are most certainly much more (that is, of course, why they were designated national parks in the first place). Those with the time and inclination to explore these parks will discover hundreds of microclimates—little worlds of their own that create unique habitats that often seem out of place in this generally arid country.

In Zion, you can see several of these microclimates along the **Riverside Walk**—there's a desert swamp where you might spot a leopard frog or two, and lush, hanging gardens on the walls as you enter the **Narrows.** You'll also find hanging gardens at **Zion's Weeping Rock,** where there is a good example of *spring lines*— water seeping through a porous rock is diverted to the surface by a layer of much harder rock.

At Bryce Canyon you'll find a moist world in the aptly named **Mossy Cave,** which is fed by a natural spring. Walking down the **Queen's Garden Trail,** you'll notice that vegetation on the north facing slopes and in narrow gullies—Douglas fir and ponderosa pines—is far different than the piñon and juniper in the sunnier areas. And there is a much cooler and wetter climate at the higher elevations in the southern section of the park—such as along the **Bristlecone Loop** and **Riggs Spring Loop Trails.**

Bryce Canyon at first seems easy to understand—it's the hoodoos—but look a bit closer and you soon come to realize that in addition to its delightful rock formations, Bryce Canyon has serene woodlands of pine where deer graze in open meadows, and dense forests of spruce and fir, where you also find the world's oldest living things—bristlecone pines. Of course, there are also the lowlands, below the rim. This is definitely a desert, yet anything but drab, with its colorful and whimsical hoodoos.

Zion has a more complicated environment. It has stupendous rock formations—even a few hoodoos of its own—but it also has the unique Narrows, a canyon carved by the Virgin River with fascinating microclimates and habitats that support plants and animals not seen elsewhere in the park. These include the rare Zion snail, found nowhere else in the world. In some ways, Zion seems to have more extremes than Bryce Canyon, ranging from delightful little pools surrounded by delicate ferns and wildflowers, to rocky, windswept ridges, where only the most determined and rugged plants and animals can survive.

The best way to explore these parks and get to know them intimately is to get away from the viewpoints and take to the trails, leaving behind the throngs, who seem to be glued to the officially designated scenic lookouts. Remember, though, that southern Utah is hot in the summer, and these parks—particularly lower-elevation Zion and some of the trails below the rim at Bryce Canyon—can be scorching desert, so be prepared as you hit the trail.

On the other hand, it is also possible to get a close-up view of nature without exerting a lot of effort. Plants and rocks are everywhere, and a variety of animals can be seen throughout both parks. To see wildlife, simply go to a quiet place—even a park campground early in the morning—and wait. Sit at the edge of a meadow or take a slow walk down almost any park path or trail—the key here is to get away from people, and especially the noise they make, and take the time to watch, wait, and listen. Nature surrounds you at both Bryce Canyon and Zion National Parks, but it doesn't necessarily advertise itself; with just a bit of patience, it can be coaxed out of hiding.

2   The Landscape

There are many reasons to visit Zion and Bryce Canyon National Parks, but what you'll find in almost all sections of both parks—and probably what you came to experience—are their intricately sculpted and often beautifully colored rock formations, from majestic, towering formations like the Great White Throne at Zion, to the delicately carved and whimsical hoodoos at Bryce Canyon. For these we can thank the geologic processes of uplifting and erosion.

The parks are located on the northwestern edge of the Colorado Plateau, a 130,000-square-mile region that covers the Four Corners area and encompasses about half of Utah, most of northern Arizona including the Grand Canyon, much of western Colorado, and the northwest corner of New Mexico. Named for the Colorado River, which is responsible for carving many of the area's scenic canyons, the Colorado Plateau began as the result of uplifting 10 to 15 million years ago. In simple terms, the large, flat beds of sedimentary rock created from different materials—or different combinations of the same materials—resulted in layers of varying densities. Forces within the earth pushed some of these sections of sediment up into the air. This is especially noticeable in places such as Zion and Bryce Canyon. Here, uplifts along geologic fault lines created high plateaus with large chunks of rock, where you can see the stripes of the different layers.

When wind and water began their inevitable erosion, layers of softer rock, such as sandstone and limestone, wore down faster than the harder layers of mudstone and shale. This created intricate and sometimes bizarre shapes. This erosion, as well as the shifting and breaking of rock, carved the sculptures of Zion and Bryce Canyon. The process almost always involves water and gravity, although wind and temperature, primarily freezing and thawing, play a role as well.

The formation called **Thor's Hammer** in Bryce Canyon, for example, owes its hammerlike shape to a variety of rock densities—the hammer section on top is harder and more resistant to erosion than the softer handle section below. Eventually, the handle will crumble and the hammerhead will come crashing to the ground.

Although there are also hoodoos similar to Thor's Hammer in Zion—mostly on the park's east side—many of Zion's rock formations appear more massive and rugged, and in some ways very different. But here, too, the rocks have simply been carved by the forces of nature, primarily water, as can be seen clearly when looking up from the bottom of the **Narrows.** This incredibly slim canyon—

How Nature Paints the Parks

The shapes are fantastic—towering monoliths, massive mesas of stone, delicate spires, intricately carved sculptures, and squat little toadstools—but what first catches our eyes are the delightful colors. What seems like an infinite variety of hues elevates these parks from geologic wonders to exquisite works of art. But where do the colors come from? What dynamic forces have meticulously painted these stone sculptures so perfectly?

The answer, simply and unpoetically put, is rust. Most of the rocks at Zion and Bryce Canyon are colored by iron, or hematite (iron oxide), either contained in the original stone or carried into the rocks by groundwater. Although iron most often creates red and pink hues, frequently seen in Zion's towering sandstone faces and Bryce Canyon's spectacular amphitheaters, it can also result in blacks, browns, yellows, and even greens. Sometimes the iron seeps into the rock, coloring it through, but it can also stain just the surface, often in vertical streaks.

Rocks are also colored by the bacteria that live on their surfaces. These bacteria ingest dust and expel iron, manganese, and other minerals, which then stick to the rock, producing a shiny black, brown, or reddish surface called desert varnish. Last, but certainly not least, is the work of water, which deposits salt as it evaporates, creating white streaks.

1,000 feet high but less than 30 feet wide in some places—was meticulously carved through Navajo sandstone by the North Fork of the Virgin River.

The most important of Zion's nine rock layers—at least as concerns its ability to create imposing rock formations—is **Navajo sandstone,** the thickest rock layer in the park, at up to 2,200 feet. The sandstone layer was created some 200 million years ago, during the Jurassic period, when most of North America was hot and dry. Movements in the earth's crust enabled a shallow sea to form over windblown sand dunes. Then minerals, including lime from the shells of sea creatures, eventually glued sand particles together to form sandstone. Later, crust movements caused the land to uplift, draining away the sea, but leaving rivers that gradually carved the relatively soft sandstone into the spectacular shapes we see today.

By comparison, Bryce Canyon is a mere babe. Its rocks were formed some 64 million years ago, created from sediments that were left behind as ancient lakes and rivers dried up, and, as at neighboring Zion, were then uplifted and exposed to the ravages of nature. Much of Bryce Canyon's rock is **limestone,** relatively soft and crumbly, which was easily eroded into the park's numerous intricate hoodoos. And these processes continue today. Even to the naked eye, it's possible to see the changes that weathering has produced on Bryce Canyon's famous **Queen Victoria** hoodoo in only the past 25 years.

3 The Flora

Great variations in elevation and the availability of water have resulted in numerous microclimates throughout these two parks. In one section, you could see desert grasses, sagebrush, and a few cacti; while in another not far away, there might be a woods of deep green where maidenhair ferns and cottonwood trees thrive. Zion National Park boasts almost 800 native species of plant life—considered the richest diversity of plants in Utah—while at Bryce Canyon the number is closer to 400. In the lower elevations, particularly in the hot, dry desert areas of Zion, you'll find cactus, mesquite, and yucca. As elevation increases, juniper and piñon are added, and eventually, in the high mountains of Bryce Canyon, you encounter a deep forest of fir and spruce, with stands of quaking aspen that turn a magnificent bright yellow each fall.

While exploring Zion, be sure to watch for spring lines and their lush hanging gardens, which you'll see clinging to the sides of cliffs. Because sandstone is porous, water can percolate down through it until a harder layer of rock stops it. At that point the water simply changes direction, moving horizontally to the rock face, where it oozes out, forming the spring line that provides life-giving nutrients to whatever seeds the wind delivers.

TREES

ASPEN   The most widely distributed tree in North America, growing from Alaska to southern Arizona, **quaking aspen** are found here above 7,500 feet elevation, mostly above the rim and in the mountains at the southern end of Bryce Canyon, and along the cliffs and plateaus at Zion. Named "quaking" for the trembling movement of the leaves at the slightest wind, aspens have white bark and almost heart-shaped green leaves that usually turn a striking yellow or gold in the fall. Deer and elk eat the twigs and leaves, while rabbits and other small mammals eat the leaves, buds, and bark.

Quaking Aspen

Bristlecone Pine

BRISTLECONE PINE   The oldest known trees—some have lived more than 4,600 years—bristlecones nearly 2,000 years old can be found at Bryce Canyon, usually along exposed, rocky slopes above 7,500 feet of elevation. Bristlecones are recognized by their very short, dark-green needles that grow all around the branch, often tightly packed, and dark-brown, cylindrical cones. The trees commonly have a gnarled, weathered appearance, due at least in part to their age and choice of environment.

Fremont Cottonwood

COTTONWOOD   A member of the willow family, cottonwoods like lots of water and are usually found along streams or other permanent water sources. The **narrowleaf cottonwood,** found along water courses in Bryce Canyon, has skinny green willowlike leaves that turn dull yellow in the fall; while the **Fremont cottonwood,** found in almost all moist areas of Zion, has large, triangular-shaped, shiny yellow-green leaves that turn bright yellow in fall.

DOUGLAS FIR   This large evergreen—some can grow as tall as 200 feet—has medium-sized, blue-green needles and fairly large cones. Birds and various mammals eat the seeds, while deer eat the foliage. It is found at most elevations in the canyons and on the plateaus at Zion National Park (you'll find good stands on the Kolob Terrace). At Bryce Canyon, you'll find Douglas fir primarily above 7,500 feet of elevation, especially in the southern part of the park.

Douglas Fir

Juniper

JUNIPER   Two types of juniper—**Rocky Mountain** and **Utah**—grow in the parks, most often in canyons and on rocky slopes. Utah juniper are usually seen at the lower and drier elevations—below the rim at Bryce Canyon—while Rocky Mountain juniper will grow throughout the parks up to 8,500 feet. The Utah juniper has a short trunk and low, spreading branches, with closely spaced, yellow-green needles; the Rocky Mountain juniper is often taller, sometimes reaching 50 feet, with slender branches and short, gray-green needles. Both have berrylike cones that are a popular food for birds and other wildlife. The Utah juniper's "berries" are a dull blue, while the "berries" of the Rocky Mountain juniper are bright blue with a white coating.

PIÑON PINE   Common throughout the southern Rocky Mountains between 5,000 and 7,000 feet of elevation, piñons are found at both parks, although mostly below the rim at Bryce Canyon. They are usually fairly small, somewhat gnarled, with rough bark and light green needles up to an inch and a half long that usually grow in bundles of two. The small, egg-shaped cones produce edible seeds, often called nuts, which are a popular food for both humans and wildlife. The piñon jay takes its name from the tree and its tasty seeds.

Piñon Pine

PONDEROSA PINE This large, impressive tree, which is found in both parks, is easily recognized by its long needles—up to 10 inches—that usually grow in bundles of three. Adult trees have orange-tinted bark that has a fragrance similar to vanilla, and large, reddish-brown cones that are round or egg-shaped. At Zion, look for the ponderosa pine along cliffs and high plateaus; it is found at Bryce Canyon on sunny slopes above and along the rim, in the campgrounds, and around Bryce Lodge.

Ponderosa Pine

SHRUBS & FERNS

MAIDENHAIR FERN A surprise in southern Utah's generally arid terrain, this moisture-loving fern, known for its delicate, lacy fronds and thin black stems, thrives in select areas of Zion National Park, near sources of water such as the Emerald Pools, and in hanging gardens, including those at Weeping Rock.

SAGEBRUSH Covering much of the American West, various types of sagebrush are found throughout Zion and Bryce Canyon. A shrub that normally grows in alkaline soil in arid areas, it can reach several feet tall if it gets sufficient water. A common food for deer and other animals, sagebrush has a fresh, pungent scent—strongest when it's wet—that is similar to the spice sage. It has tiny, gray-green leaves and sprouts small, white flowers in the fall. Three varieties grow at Bryce Canyon: **big, black,** and **fringed;** while big and **old man** grow at Zion.

Big Sagebrush

Yucca

YUCCA Not a cactus as many think, but a shrub, yuccas grow in dry, rocky areas of both parks. One of the prettiest plants of the Southwest—absolutely stunning when it's in bloom—the yucca was extremely important to early American Indians, who made baskets and sandals from its strong leaves, ate its fruits and flowers, and turned its roots into a shampoo. The plant has long, extremely tough green leaves, which have sharp spines on their leaf tips that can be quite painful to the touch. In spring or early summer the yucca produces a tall stalk of large, white flowers. You'll find the **narrow-leaf yucca** at Bryce Canyon, and the **Datil** (broad-leaf) and **Utah** varieties at Zion.

FLOWERING PLANTS

CLARET CUP CACTUS One of 14 varieties of cactus found in the desert areas of Zion National Park, the claret cup boasts one of the park's most beautiful flowers and sometimes produces its brilliant red blooms in spring, sometimes as early as March. The cactus stem (the body) is gray-green, cylindrical, 3 to 4 inches across, and covered with long, sharp, curved spines. As plants mature, numerous stems may grow, and they are stunning when covered with flowers.

Claret Cup Cactus

Columbine

COLUMBINE A member of the buttercup family, columbine come in a variety of intricate shapes and colors. Flowers have five petals, but the overall appearance can vary quite a bit. Columbine usually prefer shady, moist areas, such as Zion's hanging gardens, but will also grow in rocky canyons and open meadows. Species at Zion are the **golden columbine** (with a beautiful yellow flower) and the **western columbine** (with red and yellow flowers). In Bryce Canyon, you'll find **blue columbine** (the Colorado state flower) in meadows above 7,500 feet and in the high forest at the southern end of the park. Blooming season is late spring and early summer at Zion, and mid- to late-summer at Bryce Canyon.

LARKSPUR Another member of the buttercup family, the larkspur is represented by several families in the drier areas of both parks, blooming in summer. Flowers are small—about 1 inch across—and are blue, violet, or white.

Larkspur

Prickly Pear Cactus

PRICKLY PEAR CACTUS One of the easiest types of cactus to identify, as well as one of the most common, prickly pears have flattened paddle-shaped pads covered with spines. You'll find them throughout the drier areas of both parks, up to about 8,500 feet. Prickly pear usually bloom in late spring or early summer at Zion, a little later in Bryce Canyon, and produce pretty flowers, about 2 to 3 inches across. Flowers are mostly bright yellow, but sometimes pink or magenta. The plains and Englemann prickly pear you see at Zion are similar to the types usually encountered throughout the Southwest, with dull green pads and rigid spines an inch or so long. A bit unusual is the grizzly bear prickly pear that grows at Bryce Canyon. Although its pads are similar to other prickly pears, you can hardly see them because of what looks like long hair but is actually its spines, which are flexible, white, and sometimes up to a foot long.

SACRED DATURA   Dubbed the "Zion Lily" because of its abundance in the park, the sacred datura has large, funnel-shaped white flowers that open in the cool of night and are often closed by noon the next day. You'll see them frequently along roadsides and other areas where the soil has been disturbed, generally in dry, sandy soil below 7,000 feet elevation. Also called the Southwestern thorn apple, the sacred datura's flowers are 5 to 8 inches long and just as wide—the largest blossoms of any plant in southern Utah—and bloom from early spring through fall. Because it blossoms at night, it is also sometimes called the moon lily. *Warning:* The sacred datura is highly poisonous, and if any part of the plant is ingested it is likely to cause hallucinations, convulsions, and quite possibly death.

Sacred Datura   *Sego Lily*

SEGO LILY   Found in the drier areas below the rim in Bryce Canyon and in the canyons, cliffs, and plateaus of Zion, the sego lily has delicate white flowers, each about 1 to 2 inches wide. Flowers appear in late spring or early summer, and each is bell shaped, with three petals. The sego lily is the Utah state flower, and the state's early Mormon settlers ate the plant's bulbs when food was scarce.

4 The Fauna

Just as with these parks' plant life, elevation and availability of water determine what animals you'll see in any particular area. Zion, again, has the most diversity, with about 75 species of mammals, about 270 species of birds, and close to 30 species of reptiles and amphibians. Bryce Canyon also has plenty of wildlife to spot, though, with about 55 species of mammals, 160 species of birds, and about 15 species of reptiles and amphibians. Most of the animals in the lower elevations are those of the desert—small creatures such as lizards and snakes, kangaroo rats, rabbits, and squirrels. As the elevation increases, watch for prairie dogs, beavers, bighorn sheep, and mule deer. In the high forests of Bryce Canyon, keep an eye out for elk, pronghorn, and possibly black bear.

MAMMALS

BIGHORN SHEEP   Named for the large, curving horns on the rams, **desert bighorn sheep** are brown or light tan, with prominent white splotches on their rumps, faces, and legs. They inhabit isolated and harsh desert environments—what appear to be the most inhospitable areas. Your best chance to see bighorn sheep in this area is in the steep, rocky areas on the east side of Zion National Park. They eat a variety of grasses and shrubs—practically whatever is available—and can go without water for more than 5 days.

Bighorn Sheep

Black Bear

BLACK BEARS   Although often black in the eastern United States, black bears in the West are usually brown or even tan. The males are big, up to about 6 feet tall and weighing over 500 pounds, but the females are much smaller. Bears like wooded areas, usually below 7,000 feet elevation, and there are occasional sightings in both parks. However, rather than actually seeing a bear in the flesh (or the

The Return of the Bighorn Sheep

Although there were reports of significant numbers of desert bighorns in the area now known as Zion National Park prior to the 20th century, the population gradually declined. This was due primarily to development of the land by settlers, who blocked access to water, planted crops, and brought in livestock that not only competed with the bighorns for grazing land but also introduced diseases. Another problem for the bighorns came with construction of the Zion–Mt. Carmel Highway and Tunnel in the 1920s, which effectively chopped their range in half. Park officials estimated that by the 1930s there were about 25 bighorns in the park and believe there were none left by the late 1950s.

Reintroduction efforts began in the mid-1960s, although it was not until 1973 that a dozen desert bighorns were captured in southern Nevada and brought to the park, where they were kept in an 80-acre enclosure. By 1976 there were 22 bighorns, still trapped in the enclosure, and park service wildlife biologists decided to release 13, moving them by helicopter to an isolated canyon in the southeastern corner of the park. Unfortunately, by the next year only 4 of the 13 had survived in the wild, due in part to the deaths of some by mountain lions, and this part of the reintroduction effort was considered a failure. By 1978, the population of the bighorns that remained in the enclosure had increased to 20, and they were released into the park. Although 9 died over the course of the next year, this release was considered a success.

Today there are at least 65 bighorns at Zion, and it appears that the herd is making a successful comeback, both in terms of reproduction and range expansion. Park officials believe the park could support at least twice as many desert bighorns, but at least for the time being there are no plans to introduce more from other areas, in part because of the fear that new animals would bring in new diseases.

fur), it's more likely that you'll see signs of the bear's presence, such as decayed stumps or logs that have been torn apart for the grubs they contained, or tooth and claw marks on trees. Interestingly, bear footprints look similar to those made by humans, with the addition of a small round mark above each toe produced by the bear's claws.

CHIPMUNKS   Of the 22 species of chipmunks in North America, 21 can be found in the western United States. It is often difficult to tell one chipmunk species from another (at least for humans), but it's usually fairly easy to distinguish chipmunks from their cousins the squirrels, since chipmunks have black-and-white facial stripes while squirrels do not. Uinta, least, and cliff species of chipmunks will be found at both Bryce Canyon and Zion. The **cliff** chipmunk, which is often seen in rocky areas near cliffs, is usually the biggest of the three, sometimes reaching more than 10 inches long. The **Uinta** is usually seen scurrying about in pine and fir forests, such as those in both parks' campgrounds, while **least** chipmunks are at home in open areas of desert terrain, such as the beginning sections of the Under the Rim Trail at Bryce Canyon. All three have brown and gray fur, and black-and-white stripes on their backs (although the cliff chipmunks' stripes may be less distinct than the others), in addition to facial stripes.

Chipmunk

Coyote

COYOTES Survivors, coyotes are increasing in population throughout the United States. They are seen—or more often heard—throughout both Zion and Bryce Canyon, where they hunt rabbits, rodents, and other small animals. Tan or yellow-gray, with bushy tails, coyotes look much like domestic dogs and usually weigh 30 to 40 pounds. They can run at over 25 miles per hour, reaching 40 miles per hour for short periods. One way to easily distinguish between a dog and a coyote is that coyotes run with their tails down, while domestic dogs run with their tails up. Coyote choruses are often heard at night, consisting of a series of sharp yelps, barks, and howls.

ELK Although not believed to be full-time residents of either park, **Rocky Mountain elk** are known to be in the area and are sometimes spotted in or near the parks at the higher elevations, particularly in the fir and spruce forest at the southern end of Bryce Canyon National Park, and the Kolob Plateau in the northern part of Zion. Known for the buck's large racks of antlers, Rocky Mountain elk can reach weights of more than 1,000 pounds. Their coloring is usually brown or tan, with hints of yellow on their rumps and tails.

Elk

MOUNTAIN LIONS   These large cats, usually solid tan or beige, are also known as panthers, cougars, and pumas. They are occasionally seen in both Bryce Canyon and Zion National Parks. However, there have been more sightings in Zion than in Bryce Canyon in recent years, and it is believed that there are quite a few in the backcountry areas of Kolob Canyon. At Bryce Canyon, you are most likely to see a mountain lion in the southern part of the park, in the backcountry along the Riggs Spring Loop Trail. Since they avoid humans, your best chance of seeing one is in a remote area or along a quiet roadway late at night. Skilled hunters, mountain lions prefer to catch deer, and a single mountain lion can kill and consume a mule deer a week if deer are plentiful. They also hunt coyotes, beavers, small mammals, and birds. Mountain lions will usually stash the leftovers from their kills, covering them with brush, sticks, and leaves, for later use.

Mountain Lion   *Mule Deer*

MULE DEER The most commonly seen large animals at both parks, mule deer are often spotted near the campgrounds at Zion and along the Bryce Canyon scenic drive, especially in meadows along the edge of the forest. Considered medium-sized as deer go, mule deer are usually reddish brown in summer and gray during the winter, with patches of white on their rumps and throats year-round. However, their most distinguishing characteristic—what has given them their name—is their pair of huge, mulelike ears. Bucks can weigh up to about 450 pounds, while does usually weigh only about one-third of that.

PRAIRIE DOG These cute little critters are not dogs at all, but members of the squirrel family, making them rodents. The species at Bryce Canyon—the **Utah prairie dog**—is listed as a threatened species, which both amuses and annoys southern Utah ranchers, who consider it a pest. Utah prairie dogs are about a foot long, reddish-tan, and have small ears. Active during the day, prairie dogs live in park meadows in busy communities comprised of burrows, with mounds of dirt at each entrance. These colonies are strategically located in areas that have enough grass and other plants to sustain them, but with vegetation that is sparse and low enough for them to be able to spot predators with enough time to dart into their burrows. Prairie dogs seem to delight in alternately running about and standing at attention, making their antics popular with park visitors. *One warning, though:* The bacteria that causes bubonic plague has been found on fleas in prairie dog colonies in Bryce Canyon, so you should avoid getting too close. In any case, they bite.

Prairie Dog   *Pronghorn*

PRONGHORN Commonly seen in open fields in the vicinity of Bryce Canyon National Park—although not always within the park's boundaries—pronghorns were recently reintroduced into the area after being practically eliminated in the late 1800s and early 1900s. Sometimes called the American antelope, pronghorns are usually reddish-tan, with white on their rumps, chest, stomach, lower parts of their faces, and inner legs. Among the fastest animals in the world, pronghorns can reach speeds of 70 miles per hour, and their speed, combined with excellent eyesight, enable them to escape many of their predators.

RABBITS You'll probably see several species of rabbits while visiting Bryce Canyon and Zion National Parks. **Black-tailed jackrabbits,** easily recognized by their tall ears and black tails, are observed frequently along the cliffs at the rim of Bryce Canyon, and throughout Zion. Usually gaunt-looking with mostly gray fur, they also have large hind feet. The cute **desert cottontails** are also found at both parks, although mostly at Zion in grasslands below 5,000 feet elevation. Desert cottontails are usually a brownish gray, with black-tipped ears and their trademark tail that looks just like a little white ball of cotton. Both species are favorite foods of the coyote.

Black-Tailed Jackrabbit

Desert Cottontail

RINGTAIL Also known as miner's cats or ringtail cats, ringtails are not cats at all, but relatives of the raccoon. They have foxlike faces with big, round, dark eyes, but their most conspicuous feature is their long, bushy, black-and-white tail. The ringtail is usually about 30 inches long, and often more than half of that is tail. Although common in Zion and present, although not in abundance, at Bryce Canyon, ringtails are seldom seen because they sleep all day in caves or other quiet places and emerge only after dark, when their super-sharp claws and catlike agility enable them to catch rodents, small mammals, birds, and insects. They are also not above raiding campsites. Ringtails got their nickname "miner's cats" because in the late 1800s and early 1900s they were taken into mines, where they quickly eliminated the mouse and rat populations.

Ringtail

SQUIRRELS   Practically every visitor to Zion and Bryce Canyon National Parks will see squirrels—at Zion, there's an abundance of **white-tailed antelope** and **rock** squirrels, while the most commonly seen species at Bryce Canyon is the **golden-mantled ground** squirrel, although there are plenty of rock and **red** squirrels as well. Often confused with chipmunks, which are generally the same size, shape, and coloring as squirrels, it's really quite easy to tell them apart—chipmunks have stripes on the sides of their faces and squirrels do not. The golden-mantled ground squirrel, which seems to think it owns the Bryce Canyon campgrounds, is especially attractive, with a white stripe bordered by two black stripes along each side of its brownish-gray body, and reddish-brown or copper-colored head and shoulders.

Squirrel

BIRDS

AMERICAN DIPPER   Also called water ouzels, these birds are seen year-round in the Narrows at Zion National Park, where they dive into the Virgin River in search of aquatic insects. Mostly slate-gray, with a stocky build, short tail, and wings, they run along the river bottom underwater, and in shallow areas appear to be water-skiing on the surface.

American Dipper

Mountain Chickadee

CHICKADEE   Mountain chickadees are abundant year-round at Bryce Canyon, both below the rim and throughout the ponderosa pine forest, up to 8,500 feet elevation; and in Zion in the piñon-juniper forest, such as along Watchman Trail, as well as the higher elevations. These small birds—only about 5 inches long—have pale, gray backs, jet-black caps and eye bands, and white cheeks, eyebrows, and chests.

Bald Eagle

Golden Eagle

EAGLES   Both **golden** and **bald** eagles are seen fairly frequently at Bryce Canyon, especially near the cliffs along the rim; and occasionally at Zion, where golden eagles are sometimes spotted in the canyons and on the plateaus, while bald eagles are more commonly seen near water, including the Virgin River and its tributaries. Both species are large, with wingspans usually over 6 feet. The golden

Eagle Not Regal

At least one of America's founding fathers was less than enthusiastic about selecting the bald eagle as the symbol of the country. In 1784 Benjamin Franklin wrote to his daughter Sarah, complaining that the bald eagle is "a bird of bad moral character," and stating, "The turkey is a much more respectable bird, and withal a true original native of America."

eagle is dark—brown and black—with a light gold color on the back of its neck. The bald eagle looks much like the golden eagle when young, but it develops a white head and tail and more solidly black body as it matures. Bald eagles have yellow bills, which are larger than the dark gray bills of golden eagles. While golden eagles eat rabbits and large rodents, bald eagles generally prefer fish, which is why they are usually seen near bodies of water. A few golden eagles are year-round residents of both parks; fall through spring is the best time to see bald eagles. (See also "Turkey Vulture," below.)

HERON Large birds with long legs and necks, **great blue herons** are ideally suited for wading in the reservoirs and rivers in Zion National Park in search of a fish dinner. They will also eat insects, smaller birds, and rodents, and are sometimes seen as they migrate through the area in spring or fall. Great blue herons often stand over 4 feet tall, and have wingspans of almost 6 feet. In color, however, they are not really blue but mostly gray, with some black and white, and have a long, pointed yellow bill. Occasionally they are also seen in or near Bryce Canyon National Park.

Great Blue Heron

HUMMINGBIRDS   These colorful little birds are delightful to watch, as they hover at flowers sipping nectar, perform rambunctious aerial mating dances, or warn other hummingbirds away with tail-fanning and other displays. (You might also notice that hummingbirds can fly backward—they're the only birds known to do this.) Among the species at Zion are the **black-chinned, Costa's, broad-tailed,** and **rufous;** while at Bryce Canyon, you will most likely see the black-chinned and broad-tailed, although rufous are occasionally spotted. The most colorful among these are the rufous: The males are a startling reddish-brown with an iridescent red-orange throat, while females have green backs with areas of reddish-brown on their tails and flanks.

Black-Chinned Hummingbird

Broad-Tailed Hummingbird

JAYS   Among the noisiest and most raucous-sounding birds, jays are almost always heard before they are seen, although because of their size—sometimes a foot long—these year-round residents of both parks are easy to spot as well. **Scrub jays,** seen at numerous locations at both Zion and Bryce Canyon, often have a brilliant blue back, white or gray underneath, and a black mask. **Steller's jays** are bright blue on their lower half and flat black above, with a prominent crest on the top of their heads. **Piñon jays** are a deep blue almost all over, with a bit of white on their throats and possibly other markings.

Scrub Jay

Steller's Jay

NUTHATCHES   Seen year-round throughout both Bryce Canyon and Zion, especially at higher elevations, nuthatches are known for their ability to walk down tree trunks with their heads aimed straight down. The **white-breasted** nuthatch is the species most commonly spotted at Zion, sometimes along the upper sections of the West Rim Trail or in the Kolob Canyon area; it's also seen in various locations throughout Bryce Canyon. A white-breasted nuthatch is about 6 inches long, with a blue back; a white face, chest, and belly; and a black cap on its head. The **pygmy** nuthatch is commonly seen in the ponderosa pine forests in Bryce and occasionally observed in Zion. This tiny bird, rarely more than $4^1/_2$ inches from the tip of its beak to the tip of its tail, is bluish-gray on its back and sides, white or light gray underneath, and it has a dark cap on its head. Also frequently seen at Bryce Canyon—generally in the forests above 8,500 feet—but only occasionally at Zion are **red-breasted** nuthatches, which, not surprisingly, are recognized by their red or rust-colored chests. They have blue-gray backs and dark crowns, plus white eyebrows and a dark line behind each eye.

Piñon Jay   *Pygmy Nuthatch*

PEREGRINE FALCON   Fairly common along the cliffs just below the rim at Bryce Canyon, and occasionally seen at Zion, peregrine falcons have wingspans that often exceed 3 feet, which helps make them one of the world's fastest birds, able to exceed 200 miles per hour. They're known to breed at Zion and sometimes nest in the Weeping Rock area. Their back and wings are usually slate-gray or blue-gray, which also projects vertically down their face in bands over their eyes. The rest of their face and neck is a light gray or white, and underneath these falcons are usually a medium gray. During peregrine falcon nesting, which takes place from early spring through July, some areas at Zion National Park are off-limits to rock climbers. Pesticides drastically reduced the number of peregrine falcons in the United States in the 1950s and 1960s, and by 1970 there were only 39 breeding pairs known to exist in the continental

Although it's generally true that you'll see most animals—especially mammals—early and late in the day, finding a quiet spot can be almost as important. For instance, you're likely to see **mule deer** in Watchman Campground at Zion in midday. When practically all the campers have left for the trails or scenic drives, the deer take advantage of the quiet to stop in for a drink in the creek.

United States. But after years on the endangered species list they are on the increase again, thanks to a ban on many pesticides, and in 1999 there were sufficient numbers of the birds that they were removed from the list. Interestingly, you'll also see peregrines in cities, where they nest on tall buildings or bridges and dine on pigeons.

Peregrine Falcon

Red-Tailed Hawk

RED-TAILED HAWK   Year-round residents of both Bryce Canyon and Zion, red-tailed hawks are always on the lookout for small rodents, the mainstay of their diet. They're often seen as they glide over open areas in search of prey—watch for them over the hoodoos in Bryce Canyon—or perch in a tree at the edge of a meadow, watching for any movement in the grass. Stocky, with wingspans of about 4 feet, red-tails are named for their rust-colored tails. Their chests and faces are usually white, and their upper parts are variable, from light to dark brown.

Violet-Green Swallow

Cliff Swallow

SWALLOWS Known for their long, pointed wings and superb grace while flying, you'll often see flocks of swallows in both parks during the summer, soaring over the meadows and plateaus, and along the cliffs at the rim of Bryce Canyon. The most commonly seen species are **violet-green** swallows—pretty little birds with striking, metallic-green backs, bright violet on their tails, and white faces and lower parts. Also watch for **cliff** swallows in both parks, not only near cliffs but also in the woods along the Virgin River at Zion. Cliff swallows have mostly blue-gray upper parts, with white below, but also often have dark auburn throats and foreheads.

SWIFTS This speedy bird (thus the name) not only catches and consumes its dinner of insects while flying, but also never perches, clinging instead to trees and other vertical surfaces. **White-throated** swifts are found during the summer in the canyons and cliffs at both Zion and Bryce Canyon, often in the same areas as violet-green swallows. White-throated swifts are basically black and white—the wings, tail, and top of the head are black; the lower face, throat, and most of the chest are white.

White-Throated Swift

TURKEY VULTURE   Bird-watchers in both Zion and Bryce Canyon have reported sightings of turkey vultures, also called buzzards, which are about the same size as eagles and, when flying, are sometimes mistaken for golden eagles. The main visual difference is that the turkey vulture has a red head, and unlike the golden eagle it can glide seemingly forever without flapping its wings, riding on columns of warm air known as thermals.

Turkey Vulture

REPTILES & AMPHIBIANS

CANYON TREE FROG   Often camouflaged among rocks near pools and streams in Zion National Park's side canyons, the canyon tree frog is generally olive, gray, or brown with indistinct dark patches on its back. From $1^{1}/_{4}$ to $2^{1}/_{4}$ inches long, it often has a light spot below its eye. During its spring mating season, you can often hear a lively chorus of tree frogs.

Canyon Tree Frog

Rattlesnake

GREAT BASIN RATTLESNAKE   A subspecies of the western rattlesnake, the Great Basin rattlesnake is found both above and below the rim at Bryce Canyon, and in most areas of Zion. Generally they hibernate in winter, so you will most likely encounter them only from April through October. Sometimes growing to more than 5 feet long, they are usually gray or light brown with dark patches on their backs. They have wide, triangular-shaped flat heads, and bony, interlocking segments on their tails, which produce a buzzing or hissing noise when shaken—this usually happens when the snake is agitated. Each time the snake sheds its skin, which can occur up to five times a year, the rattle gets a new segment. These snakes are highly poisonous, but usually only attack humans when they feel threatened. Because they are mainly nocturnal, those walking in isolated areas at night should use flashlights to avoid stepping on them.

MOUNTAIN SHORT-HORNED LIZARD These little lizards—usually between 2 and 4 inches long—are found in abundance in a variety of habitats in Bryce Canyon National Park and at higher elevations at Zion. They are active mostly during the day, and their diet consists mainly of ants, but they will also eat other insects and even small snakes. Mountain short-horned lizards have a broad, flat body, short tail, and short horns on the back of their heads. They are usually a reddish brown, with darker spots on their backs.

Short-Horned Lizard

NORTHERN SAGEBRUSH LIZARD Commonly seen on trails below the rim at Bryce Canyon National Park and in the dry, open areas of rocks and sagebrush at Zion, the northern sagebrush lizard is slim, at least compared to the mountain short-horned lizard discussed above, and brown to grayish-green in color; the males have blue markings on their bellies. This lizard may also have stripes of various shades of brown or light tan running the length of its body.

INVERTEBRATES

ZION SNAIL One creature unique to Zion National Park is the Zion snail, which you'll only find clinging to wet canyon walls in a 4-mile section of the Narrows along the Virgin River—the Riverside Walk as it enters the Narrows is a good place to see them. The walls are kept moist by seeps and springs, which also nurture hanging gardens. This tiny snail, complete with shell, is a mere $1/8$ inch or less across, and to the naked eye appears to be just a dark brown or black speck on a shiny, wet wall. They hold on to the slick walls with a suction-cup foot, which in proportion to the creature's size is the biggest foot of any snail, a phenomenon that has caused some park rangers to refer to the Zion snail as "our little bigfoot." Please do not attempt to touch these fragile creatures.

5   The Ecosystem

So far, Zion and Bryce Canyon National Parks have managed to escape most of the serious ecological problems that plague some of America's other national parks, such as air and water pollution from nearby cities, adjacent mining, and extreme overcrowding (with its resultant air and noise pollution from automobiles). Still, there is the threat of air pollution from power plants across the Colorado Plateau, and the park service has additional concerns over how Bryce Canyon and Zion National Parks can be best managed to both preserve their often delicate ecosystems and produce a rewarding experience for park visitors.

Presently, visitors to both Zion and Bryce Canyon can still get away from humanity fairly easily by heading out onto park trails or into the backcountry, and they can still find relatively unspoiled areas there. To preserve these unspoiled areas and their ecosystems, there are increasing efforts in both parks to make visitors understand the need for zero-impact visitation, or as close as people can get to that short of staying home. In most cases, people are getting the message and are doing their best to stay on trails, not pollute water or drop trash, and certainly not to disturb the parks' plants and animals. In addition, shuttle bus systems have been implemented at both parks to help relieve traffic congestion and parking problems.

One issue that is expected to take on more importance in the years to come—and over which the National Park Service has little control—is increasing development in nearby communities. Major hotels have recently been built in Springdale, just outside Zion; and some degradation to Bryce Canyon's delightful night sky is feared from development of a large 24-hour gas station and a new motel just outside that park's entrance.

Meanwhile, within park boundaries the main issue—both now and for the future—is overcrowding, and how it affects the variety of habitats that support a vast array of plant and animal life. Officials of the National Park Service have taken the position that they do not want to limit the number of people who visit the parks, and in late 1997, Department of the Interior Secretary Bruce Babbitt said, "The problem isn't too many people, it's too many cars." Babbitt was talking about the planned ban on private motor vehicles at Zion, plus similar plans at Grand Canyon and Yosemite National Parks. Added Rodney Slater, Secretary of Transportation, "It's time for us to build a transit system for the 21st century that allows us to spend more time sighting bears than looking for a parking spot."

This issue of how the parks can handle an increasing number of visitors brings to mind the question of the entire philosophy of the National Park Service, which essentially is to accomplish two goals simultaneously—preserve resources and promote visitor enjoyment. But which is more important: protecting the plants, animals, and geologic formations that make these parks the special places they are, or helping people enjoy these very same plants, animals, and geologic formations?

In an interview with the nonprofit **National Parks and Conservation Association,** published in the November/December 1997 issue of the association's magazine, *National Parks,* National Park Service Director Robert Stanton said that resource protection should take precedence over the public's enjoyment. But he added, "It is a management decision to discern what level of visitor use can be accommodated without harming in an irreparable way the resources . . . . It's an easy thing to describe; it's a difficult thing to accomplish."

Essentially, the question is how far should parks go to accommodate their visitors—the people who pay the entrance and user fees and in most cases the tax dollars that fund the parks—and at what point does each and every visitor's impact become unacceptable? It's a tightrope for park managers and a debate both within and outside the park service that will not be settled soon, if ever.

Index

See also separate Accommodations and Restaurant indexes, below.

ACCOMMODATIONS